e pluribus unum

The Making of Burson-Marsteller

How a diverse collection of
men and women on five
continents worked in harmony
to create the world's largest
public relations firm

Harold Burson

Burson·Marsteller

230 Park Avenue South
New York, New York 10003

Book and cover design by Marsteller

Printed in the United States of America

*For my wife and partner for fifty-six years, Bette Foster Burson,
who shared more than half the load while I wandered the world.*

*And for our sons, Scott and Mark, their wives, Wendy and Ellen,
and our five grandchildren, Allison, Esther, Wynn, Holly and Kelly.*

A WORD ABOUT THE TITLE

From the time Burson-Marsteller began its phenomenal growth, I have maintained that literally hundreds of men and women of many nationalities and varied talents are the people who made it happen and deserve the credit. I was especially blessed that so many of high competence and steadfast commitment dedicated from fifteen to forty years of their lives to the company I co-founded with Bill Marsteller.

The guy whose name is in front of the hyphen is grateful for their support. Without them, it wouldn't have happened – Burson-Marsteller would not have developed as not only a large firm but also one with a singularly unique culture of caring and sharing in the thirty-plus countries where we have offices.

— Harold Burson

Contents

Foreword

A Brief Retrospective by One Present at the Creation

When my small firm of five people transformed into Burson-Marsteller on March 2, 1953*, the odds were that the new company would not be around fifty years later. Back then only a few public relations firms survived their founders.

Nor at age 32, chances were no greater that I would be alive a half century later.

Certainly, I had no idea the company I started would grow to more than 2,000 people in thirty countries on five continents. Or that in 1983 it would become the world's largest public relations firm – a few years later referred to as "the standard against which all other public relations firms are measured."

Not bad for an upstart that began life doing what was then called "industrial" publicity.

*For about 20 years we called ourselves Burson-Marsteller Associates. During the post-World War II era the word "associates" was used by many small professional service firms to indicate they were larger than the one or two names on the door.

⎯⎯⎯◦∞∞◦⎯⎯⎯

On the surface, Bill Marsteller and I were as different as any two people could be. He was tall and gangly, six-foot-three versus my five-foot-six. He was methodical and studied in everything he did. To those who didn't know him well, he projected a stern, even forbidding, demeanor. He was a superb writer who communicated regularly through a series of memos, usually biweekly, that are now collector's items and the content of two books.

But we were alike in many ways. We shared the same values and some of the same interests. Like me, he was a so-called child of the depression. He valued money and was not prone to spend it foolishly, either his own or his clients'. He believed in "a day's work for a day's pay." Every employee in every U.S. office signed a time sheet until the day he retired in 1979. He was a perfectionist: his most memorable speech – he was as forceful a speaker as he was skillful a writer – was titled "The Pursuit of Excellence." His commitment to clients was total. He prided himself – as did I – on sharing ownership of the business with employees and on the company's reputation as one of the best places to work. In particular, he valued support staff – the secretaries, and bookkeepers, and receptionists and mailroom staff – those prone to get short shrift in a business where professional staff is king of the roost.

Bill Marsteller's primary role was as CEO of Marsteller Advertising, the premier business-to-business advertising agency in the world for more than three decades. As it expanded into consumer packaged goods, it turned out some highly creative work, including two all-time top 50 television commercials on view at the Museum of Television and Radio. One was the "Crying Indian" for Keep America Beautiful; the other for Dannon Yogurt featuring a 92-year-old Republic of Georgia native who credited yogurt for both his and his mother's longevity.

Bill Marsteller had a second role. He was CEO of what was, in effect, a holding company that served as parent for our two businesses: advertising and public relations. Although they operated independently of one another, they usually were housed on separate floors in the same building and had their own telephone numbers while sharing a common switchboard. They had the same office hours, observed the same holidays and the same administrative and personnel policies and procedures. This part of the business was Bill Marsteller's domain, and he was a strong unifying symbol even while respecting the differing requirements of the two operating entities.

At the professional level, Bill Marsteller had little involvement in day-to-day activities of our public relations business except where we shared clients with whom he was closely associated, primarily Rockwell. He was a strong proponent of what we then called "total communications" – a precursor to today's "integrated communications." Our experience was that it worked well with business-to-business clients, especially where advertising and public relations reported to the same person. But joint clients accounted for a decreasing percentage of Burson-Marsteller's total revenue from the 1970s onward as we expanded as a full service public relations/public affairs business. When Bill Marsteller retired, about twenty percent of B-M's revenues came from clients that employed both disciplines. He moved to Palm Beach, Florida, when he retired. He died in 1987 at age 73.

As our reputation spread around the world, I have tried to understand the dynamics that have honed our singular differentiation. Even as the public relations business has become more competitive and we can no longer claim the largest revenues, our reputation remains at a high level. That positioning is the result of an evolutionary process that dates from our founding.

1. Of the many gifted professionals we hired during our first two decades, about a hundred stayed fifteen to forty years. This group of long-timers served as a "cadre" that provided the continuity that nurtured our special culture. They also developed a uniform methodology that delivers the same high quality service globally. While highly capable as individual practitioners, our "core group" was even more spectacular as a team. The whole was greater than the sum of its parts. As Jim Dowling aptly put it, "we prize the individual, we celebrate the team." People working together in harmony and with mutual respect became a Burson-Marsteller hallmark palpable to employees and clients alike.

2. We worked hard to create a strong sense of family and it paid off. We worked hard at being unencumbered by areas of specialization, national boundaries and distance, or profit center financial accountability. We were unique at creating teams and task forces from around the region and around the world. Our goal was winning business and best serving the client. Our Vision and Values statement in the late 1980s read, "we accept blame individually; we take credit collectively." We cared about one another and we shared with one another. Corny? Maybe. But it worked!

3. Our single culture worldwide did not happen by chance. It came about

because we were strong believers in organic growth. When we started an office in a country new to us, we seeded it with experienced B-Mers who hired and trained local staff. We seldom entered a new country by acquiring an existing firm. Additionally, we invested in bringing our people together for training. This resulted in widespread global networking and even numerous inter-company marriages! B-M people, as much as the décor and the methodology, were of the same pattern around the world.

4. Even when we had minimal justification to do so, we positioned ourselves as leaders. We were not afraid to take risks – we made "outside the envelope" recommendations to clients or we dared to open an office in Europe when annual revenues were barely half a million dollars. We were early adopters of multimedia for new business presentations when Carousel projectors were still a novelty. We used so many 35-mm slides we became the second largest slide maker in New York. We were first to install a broadcast quality television studio with satellite uplink and downlink. We were the first public relations firm to do hourly billing (which has both its good and its not so good aspects!), the first to own a 360 IBM computer, the first to produce an infomercial, and the first with a word processing network serving all our offices. We were pioneers in helping clients with litigation support, the first to do crisis simulation, the first to build a crisis management practice, and the first full-service firm to establish a healthcare practice.

Though I get most of the credit, the fact is, I had the support of literally scores of professional associates, male and female, of many nationalities possessed of a staggering range of expertise. Three who worked along side me for most of the thirty-five years I served as Chief Executive Officer merit special recognition.

Buck Buchwald, Jim Dowling and Bob Leaf

Starting in 1951, Elias (Buck) Buchwald was my closest professional associate. From the beginning of Burson-Marsteller, he was our professional conscience and the stern taskmaster who set high standards both qualitatively and quantitatively. A graduate chemical engineer, he got the work out, the one most responsible for our early differentiation as tops among business-to-business public relations firms. He was the "Mr. Inside" alongside my "Mr. Outside," the "tough cop" who balanced my role as the "nice cop." No one played a more central role in establishing the Burson-Marsteller culture than Buck Buchwald. He retired just a few years ago and continues to have an office at 230 Park Avenue South.

Jim Dowling joined us in 1965 as an account executive. He came to my notice when I learned he was working all night publishing a daily newspaper, delivered at breakfast-time, for a client seeking attention at a major industry convention. He next led our work for Owens-Corning, a client we got in the late 1960s that enabled us to demonstrate Burson-Marsteller was much more than a gaggle of industrial publicists. Jim's reward was a promotion to general manager of our New York office succeeding Buck Buchwald. He demonstrated his commitment when I asked him to move to Chicago, a then-troubled office that had not yet found its way. Jim's next move in 1980 returned him to New York in charge of all U.S. operations and two years later as Chief Operations Officer worldwide. He succeeded me as Chief Executive Officer in 1988. Jim, more than anyone, made Burson-Marsteller "seamless" – one interconnected enterprise operating to a single standard worldwide. Jim retired in Florida in 1999 after bringing order to our Latin American operation.

Bob Leaf was hired in 1957, our first trainee. He transferred to Europe in 1965 to lead our new Brussels office. In 1968, when we went to London, he moved there to head what we called Burson-Marsteller International, the umbrella company for our overseas offices, then three in number and destined to grow. Most probably, I had more face time with Bob as we traveled the world establishing Burson-Marsteller offices than with any other of my principal associates. Together we learned the meaning of multiculturalism as Bob fashioned and led what is still regarded as the best international public relations network in the world. Bob retired on his 40th anniversary and continues as a consultant in London.

I am proud indeed to have been able to grow old amidst such people – more than 20,000 who, at one time or another, in one part of the world or another, all treasure their days at Burson-Marsteller as a very special experience.

It has been a great ride!

— *Harold Burson*
February 2004

Chapter 1

Prepping for a Career in Public Relations: My First Twenty-five Years

The history of Burson-Marsteller is, to some degree, a reflection of my personal experiences – what I learned growing up in Memphis, attending the University of Mississippi, reporting for a daily newspaper, traveling with the CEO of a large firm of engineers/builders, and serving as both soldier and journalist in the U.S. Army in Europe during and after World War II. This is a brief account of my first 25 years – years that had a profound influence on those that followed.

My parents had lived in the United States barely a year when I was born on February 15, 1921. They had emigrated from Leeds, in Yorkshire, to Memphis, where kinsmen had settled pre-World War I. My father, a victim of the first poison gas attack by the Germans at Ypres in 1916, served five years in the British Army in France and Belgium. That heritage gave me an international outlook that remained with me through the years. A Southerner by birth – which I admit to, to this day! – I did not grow up in a traditional Southern household.

My earliest memory is of starting school. I was six years old, a first-grader for all of two days, when an older person entered the classroom, spoke to the teacher and beckoned me to come forward. Told to fetch my belongings, I was led to another classroom. Before the end of the day I learned I was now in the second grade. The next day I remember taking a test (years later I learned it was a Stanford-Binet IQ test). Finally, I was directed to still another classroom, this time the third grade, where I remained the rest of the school year.

My father – who didn't quite finish high school – taught me to read when I was three. He used the Memphis morning newspaper, *The Commercial Appeal,* as a text – first the big type in the advertisements, then the headlines, finally the news stories. Most likely, I was the only six-year-old third-grader in all the U.S. who could name President Coolidge's cabinet and the nine Supreme Court justices. But I had a problem, in fact, a big problem: I couldn't do the cursive writing that was used for all classroom assignments. Printed block letters were taboo. The teacher gave me a year to learn penmanship. I remember it as one of the most difficult tasks I have ever undertaken.

I went to the same high school as Elvis Presley – he was there fifteen years later. Early in the school year, the teacher responsible for the school newspaper asked for volunteers. That teacher became my first mentor. She gave me choice assignments and critiqued my writing, and she chose me to be the Humes High reporter for the school page in the Sunday edition of *The Commercial Appeal.* That was perhaps the first career-defining moment of my then-young life.

Rather than mail my article, I walked two miles to hand-deliver it to the school page editor. I was the only school reporter to do this, and he rewarded me by editing my article word-by-word, line-by-line and sharing with me what was good and what was not so good. As the school year came to a close, he asked me if I wanted a summer job as a copy boy. The pay was $10 dollars a week. After the first week I decided that working on a newspaper would be my life's work.

I went to the University of Mississippi because I could earn enough as a "stringer" for *The Commercial Appeal* to pay tuition and living expenses. A "stringer" is a reporter who gets paid by the column inch. My income averaged $60 a month, sufficient in those depression days to cover my college costs. Even as a freshman, my job gave me a lot of visibility, including an association with the chancellor, the head football coach and other campus leaders. The highlight of my reportorial experience at Ole Miss was an interview in 1939 with William Faulkner, an Oxford resident whose home, Rowan Oaks, was a short walk from the campus. Faulkner had just returned from three years as a screenwriter in

Hollywood. He went there because he needed the money. My front-page story in *The Commercial Appeal*, the first Faulkner interview in several years, was picked up by the Associated Press and appeared in newspapers across the country. Joseph Blotner's definitive biography on Faulkner, published in 1974, devotes two pages to an account of how I got the interview and what Faulkner told me.

Half way through my junior year, the director of the Ole Miss News Bureau, the school publicity department, was fired for wrapping his Ford Roadster around an ancient oak tree in front of the administration building. Intoxicated at the time of the accident, he was dismissed from his News Bureau job while still in the hospital recuperating from minor injuries. The chancellor asked me to serve as acting director until he could find a successor. The salary – $75 a month – was appealing and I accepted. The principal function of the News Bureau was cranking out "home towners," brief news stories sent to daily and weekly hometown newspapers reporting on student achievements such as getting elected to honorary fraternities or making the dean's list. The purpose was to give parents bragging rights while encouraging high school seniors to apply to Ole Miss.

This was my first experience in anything resembling public relations. Also, it was my first time supervising people – six students who gathered news and wrote and processed releases. The student employees were actually part of a federal government program to help young men and women go to college, the National Youth Administration. It enabled them to work forty hours a month for 25 cents an hour. (Nowadays it's difficult to believe that $10 a month made much difference, but it covered cafeteria meals for three weeks.) Shortly after taking the job, I began developing feature articles about Ole Miss and sending them around the state. We also organized a speakers bureau – the first components of what I would later learn was a public relations "program." I held the job for three semesters and believe this unintended responsibility was the most valuable aspect of my college experience.

Because of my association with *The Commercial Appeal* – two years part-time in high school and four years in college, including summers when I worked as a cub reporter in the sports department and on the city desk writing obituaries – I never thought about working elsewhere after graduation in May 1940. If I had had the financial resources to do so, I probably would have tried to get a news job in New York. During the era when I was growing up, people who fancied themselves writers wanted to go to New York or Hollywood. But I knew for certain that I had a job waiting for me at *The Commercial Appeal,* and I harbored a never-spoken hope that someday I would somehow migrate to New York.

The Commercial Appeal was actually a regional paper serving West Tennessee, North Mississippi and East Arkansas, in addition to the city of Memphis. It had a number of small "bureaus" that covered the rural areas where it had substantial circulation. Newly hired reporters were sent to one or more of these bureaus their first year. I was assigned first to Dyersburg, Tenn., and, in November, 1940, to Jackson, Tenn. Within two weeks I was covering a news story that literally changed my life.

The War Department decided to build a mammoth ammunition plant about seventy miles northeast of Memphis, within the area I covered as Jackson bureau manager. Known as the Wolf Creek Ordnance Plant, it was one of the largest construction projects ever undertaken in that part of the country, and one of the first in the national defense program prior to our entry in World War II. Since my newspaper was the principal news medium, I was important to all parties to this gigantic project – an undertaking that would cost in excess of a billion dollars in today's currency.

The story gained national attention because of a labor dispute whose resolution would likely set a pattern for future defense construction projects. The dispute arose because the engineer-builder was committed to using union labor in an area where construction sites were invariably "open shop" or non-union. Local job seekers and sub-contractors – and the politicians who represented them – protested that "outsiders" would get "all the high-paying jobs."

It was apparent early on that the union was more adept than the contractor and the Corps of Engineers in responding to the media (including, or mainly, me!). To remedy this situation, the owner of the Cleveland/New York firm selected to design and build the facility, H.K. Ferguson, whom I had interviewed several weeks earlier, asked me if I could get a two- or three-month leave of absence to handle press relations for "this important national defense project." While this was a surprising offer, I reflexively identified it as the ticket to New York I had long yearned for. On hearing my salary was $25 a week, he quickly said, "we'll double that – and give you full-time use of an automobile." Before leaving him my mind was made up to take the job. As added insurance, my editor gave me the leave of absence with the observation, "I bet you'll never come back."

The labor "crisis" was resolved in three weeks and media interest in Wolf Creek quickly dissipated. I busied myself for two months publishing a mimeographed employee newsletter and sent word to the CEO who hired me that I thought my services were no longer needed. He telephoned that he would soon visit Wolf Creek and had a proposition for me to consider. He wanted me to join his headquarters staff and suggested "the best way to learn our business is as my traveling assistant" and "while doing that, you can look after our company publicity." A week later I took my first airplane trip – Memphis to Cleveland, via Chicago. I was twenty years old and my new salary was $300 a month – plus travel expenses.

From August 1941 until December 1943, I had a job that I have always regarded as my equivalent of a Harvard M.B.A. Among The Ferguson Company's clients were such corporate giants as RCA, Procter & Gamble, Union Carbide, Corning Glass, Ford and Firestone. It designed and built part of the Oak Ridge plant that produced the fissionable material for the first atom bomb, and it designed and built all of the Army's Chemical Warfare Service facilities including Fort Detrick, the development and production center for bacterial and biological warfare agents. The company's offices were in Cleveland, New York and Washington. At any time during my tenure, it was engaged in up to fifty major construction projects on sites that spanned the continent. I was traveling with the man who started the company and made it one of the world's most highly regarded firms of industrial engineers/builders.

My job consisted of handling travel arrangements – at a time when all restaurant and hotel bills and air and rail transportation charges were paid for in cash and most travel reservations required a government-issued priority. I was keeper of the boss's calendar, in effect his scheduler and gatekeeper. I handled his incoming mail and was responsible for its disposition. I attended many of his meetings with CEOs and government officials. I was both facilitator and confidante of a competent CEO whose example had a lasting impact on me.

Additionally, I began calling on business writers at the New York, Cleveland and Washington newspapers and *The Wall Street Journal.* I also made it my business to know the editors of trade publications covering the broad spectrum of industries represented by the firm's clientele. My most notable achievement as the company's publicist was a front-page story in *The New York Times* on the first synthetic rubber produced in the United States in the spring of 1943. The Ferguson Company designed and built the plant for Firestone and it went into production a month ahead of schedule. The story also made *LIFE* magazine and my boss got a personal letter of congratulations from President Franklin D. Roosevelt who read the article in *The New York Times.*

For two years, I received draft deferments because I worked for a critical defense contractor. There is little doubt that I could have remained a civilian for the duration. However, I was determined to wear a uniform before war's end. I remember, as a child, hearing my father and his World War I veteran friends slur neighbors who had not been in the service by referring to them as "slackers." I believed that post-World War II careers in business would be strongly affected by one's military record. In mid-1943, I made several efforts to sign up for one of the Army and Navy programs leading to a commission. I passed the written and oral tests but failed the physical examination because I did not have 20/20 eyesight uncorrected. In mid-November, I asked my boss not to request another draft deferment for me. Since we had spoken about this earlier, he supported my position and assured me that my job would be waiting for me when the war was over. We agreed that I would work through the end of 1943.

Three weeks later the man I worked for suffered a sudden fatal heart attack. I knew on first hearing the news that my business career would undergo a big change. Almost immediately, I was asked to postpone my departure for an additional month. I was needed to "clean up the loose ends" of an executive who was always on the move, filling his briefcase with notes for future action – salary increases, promotions, transfers, birthdays and anniversaries to be remembered, and one of a highly personal nature to me: forgiving a $3,000 loan from the company which enabled my parents in Memphis to make the down payment on a home. But I knew that I did not want to return to the company as an employee.

My military service as an enlisted man started in March 1944. Perhaps because I worked for a firm of engineer/builders, I was assigned to an engineer combat group at Camp McCoy, Wis., for basic training. In August, I was on a troopship bound for Liverpool and, by train, headed to the resort town of Bournemouth on England's south coast. Three weeks later my unit crossed the English Channel in an LST (Landing Ship Tank), landed routinely at Utah Beach and, after a three-hour ride in an Army truck, pitched tents amidst the hedgerows in Normandy. We then joined the Ninth U.S. Army and made our way across France and Belgium, into the province of Limburg in the southeast corner of Holland and, starting February 24, 1945, across Germany all the way to the Rhine opposite Düsseldorf.

In early April, I was granted a long-delayed transfer to the Press and

Psychological Warfare Detachment of the U.S. 12th Army Group. My job was monitoring shortwave radio news and writing a mimeographed news summary for the officer's mess at U.S. Fifteenth Army headquarters in the small intact spa/kurhaus town, Bad Neuenahr, north of Koblenz. I was there when the war in Europe ended on May 8, 1945, and I knew I would not have enough points to be discharged from the service until the following May. Perhaps because war's end was both a time to rejoice and reflect, I wrote my former employer's new CEO, Kingsley Ferguson, the son of the founder with whom I had had so close a relationship, that I wanted to start my own public relations firm when I finished my army service. I also expressed the hope that his company would be my first client. Within a month, I got my answer. He wrote "we'll do it."

My rationale for starting my own business was that in my numerous contacts with business and trade editors, I learned that there were few publicists who specialized in representing what we today call business-to-business clients. Since I had no desire to return to a company where I had had so unique a role with the CEO, I decided my next career move was to settle in New York and commit myself to a career in public relations.

Hoping to spend my remaining year in the army productively (and, admittedly, hoping to avoid a transfer to the Pacific where the war with Japan was being fought with great fury), I negotiated a transfer to the news staff of American Forces Network (AFN), the Europe-wide military radio network. The most appealing aspect of my new assignment was that I would be stationed in Paris. I arrived in early July and remained five months until I was chosen to be AFN's chief correspondent at the Nuremberg Trial for the 20 major Nazi war criminals starting November 20. For the next five months I was in the Palace of Justice courtroom, an observer of the Nazi party leadership that included Goering, Hess, von Ribbentrop, Keitel, Jodl and others who plotted World War II.

My coverage of the trial consisted of a fifteen-minute broadcast every night the court was in session. I was one of two hundred correspondents who flocked to Nuremberg, among them Walter Cronkite (then with United Press) and Howard K. Smith, the CBS reporter who remained a lifelong friend. My report reached almost a million U.S. troops still in Europe as well as several million English-speaking Europeans, including thousands of Germans who regarded American Forces Network as their most credible news source. A typical broadcast described courtroom proceedings for five or six minutes, followed by an interview with someone with an unusual job at the trial – the chief jailer, the prison psychiatrist, the head of the translation service (the trial was conducted in four languages), the keeper of the documents and even the Chief U.S. Prosecutor, Justice Robert Jackson. In total, I wrote about seventy-five broadcasts and was able to save the original scripts. It makes me proud – more so in later years than when it was happening – that I never received an adverse comment from anyone in the military chain of command protesting anything I reported.

As the defendants were completing their testimony, I left Nuremberg at the end of March and took my first furlough since being inducted in the army. I spent most of April in Paris not knowing when or even whether I would ever return to what I still regard as the world's most enchanting city. In mid-May, I made my way to Le Havre where I boarded a Liberty cargo ship bound for New York and home. Outfitted and supplied to accommodate three hundred returning soldiers, only a hundred passengers were aboard. For ten glorious days on an ocean as smooth as a baby's bottom, we gorged ourselves on eggs, milk, ice cream and sirloin steak. It was a first for all us GIs since leaving the U.S. On May 26, 1946, we sailed into New York harbor, the Statue of Liberty a welcome sight that most of us saw through misted eyes. Three days later, on May 29, I was once again a civilian ready to pursue my dream to begin life anew as a public relations consultant in New York.

Chapter 2

M y name has been so closely identified with Burson-Marsteller for so long that even some of my close business associates and friends are unaware that I set up and managed my own public relations firm in New York for six years before I met Bill Marsteller. The H. K. Ferguson Company, a leading industrial engineer/builder, was my "bread and butter" account – the one that paid the rent and other expenses. My original staff was me and a part-time stenographer. When my firm became the nucleus of Burson-Marsteller, we had five people and a dozen companies and trade/professional associations as clients.

Managing a small growing business, I believe, prepared me for my future role at Burson-Marsteller. It gave me both a broad range of experience and confidence. As a sole entrepreneur, there was no alternative to my doing everything necessary to satisfy clients – contact, media placement, writing programs, even compiling mailing lists, addressing envelopes and getting news releases to the post office on time. On the business side, I was responsible for new business, seeing bills went out promptly, hiring and (occasionally) firing, and filing tax returns. As the business of public relations has matured and moved toward specialization (corporate/financial, healthcare, media relations, crisis communications, etc.), I look back favorably on those days when young professionals were trained as generalists and had to respond to all kinds of situations. That was a fertile breeding ground for well-rounded "renaissance" people.

My first business appointment after resuming life as a civilian in New York was with Guy B. Panero, a former Ferguson executive who, while I was overseas, purchased a firm that designed mechanical and electrical systems for high-rise office buildings, hotels, hospitals and other institutional buildings. One of my early mentors at Wolf Creek Ordnance plant in Tennessee, Guy gave me lesson 101 on starting a business. His reputation in construction circles stemmed from his role as chief design engineer for Rockefeller Center, even today one of the most widely acclaimed building projects ever undertaken. Unexpectedly, he asked me to publicize his recently acquired business, which, fortunately, did not compete with Ferguson. We agreed on a $500 monthly retainer, which he paid in advance. Equally important, he offered me office space and part-time secretarial and telephone service. That enabled Harold Burson Public Relations to open for business on the seventeenth floor of the Graybar Building, 420 Lexington Avenue, on August 6, 1946. A week later my printed stationery arrived.

My association with Guy Panero soon led to other small-fee construction clients. The New York Society of Consulting Engineers was the first, followed shortly by the New York Chapter of the American Institute of Architects. He introduced me to the builder of Rockefeller Center, John W. Harris, and his company became a client. While clients mainly wanted to see their names in print, I also wrote new business proposals and presentations – experience that served me well in later years. Admittedly, these clients were not in the same league as the *FORTUNE* 500 clients I would eventually work for. Monthly fees ranged from $250 to $750 per month, but their demands were modest, their expectations reasonable and they paid their bills. My income was more than it would have been had I taken a job with Ferguson or some other employer.

After six months, I had enough business to support a secretary, a part-time assistant and my own modest office. While searching for space, I learned that another Ferguson alumnus, a labor relations consultant, had a one-room office in the original General Motors Building in New York at West 57th Street and Broadway, now the *Newsweek* building. He shared the office with an insurance agent and a private investigator who worked from their homes and used the office only as a mailing address. For $150 a month, it became my office. About 12 feet wide and 20 feet deep, it accommodated three desks and a mimeograph machine that reproduced news releases. When I met Bill Marsteller, I had a slightly larger office in the New York Daily News Building at 220 East 42nd Street.

Concurrent with my move to a new office, I was in the process of getting married. In March 1947, Bette Foster entered my life. She and a girlfriend who had been a "pen pal" when I was a soldier in Europe, "happened to be in the neighborhood" of the renovated tenement where I lived on East 61st Street and "decided to ring the bell." On October 30, seven months after we met, Bette and I were married. A graduate of the prestigious Katherine Gibbs Secretarial School, she quit her job in the promotion department of Republic Pictures and joined me as full-time secretary/office manager.

About the same time, I hired my first professional staff associate, Roy Heatly, a young news writer I worked with at AFN-Frankfurt. His goal was to enroll at Columbia University following his Army service. Knowing I would be in New York, I suggested he "keep in touch." In September he matriculated at Columbia and joined me as a part-time employee.

My tax returns for the next five years show modest year-to-year increases in income that reflected slow, but steady, growth. My circle of business friends also grew. At a time when newspaper reporters and trade magazine editors welcomed being entertained, I bought lunch for a client or a reporter/editor almost every day. I also joined organizations that enabled me to meet new people in business, public relations and the media. Though not actively seeking a partner or to merge my business with another firm, I was not averse to doing either if the opportunity arose. (In 1951, I was offered a partnership in a prestigious medium-sized firm to head press relations; I turned it down because I thought the job was too limiting.)

Meanwhile, I got a lot of satisfaction knowing that clients valued my work. From the beginning, I was treated as an equal by executives twice my age. I was especially flattered when they shared confidences with me that they chose not to discuss with their day-to-day associates. Even at that early stage of my career, I served as a "sounding board" for client CEOs. Specifically, I recall two occasions where I had a role in helping a CEO choose his successor. My recollection of those early experiences was that I did a lot more listening than talking. In the years that followed, I came to understand that listening to what a client was saying is lesson one for the would-be adviser/counselor.

My clients were engaged in interesting activities, several with major roles in the then-new nuclear age. Brookhaven National Laboratories on Long Island was a big Ferguson project, designed to research peaceful applications of the atom and frequently in the news. Later, I participated in the formation of Walter Kidde

Nuclear Laboratories, headed by a distinguished Manhattan Project physicist who helped design the Oak Ridge plant that produced uranium 235 for the first atomic bomb. During the period of hysteria about the threat of nuclear war, the U.S. Atomic Energy Commission contracted with Kidde to design a prototype shelter that would protect a typical American family in a nuclear attack. Kidde came up with an underground Quonset hut-shaped structure with an earth covering eight to ten feet deep, equipped with sleeping quarters and sufficient food and water for 72 hours and air filtration equipment. *LIFE* magazine gave it two pages, one of the five *LIFE* stories I placed in my first six years in business. The Panero firm had a contract with the Army Corps of Engineers to design prototypes of underground factories. That also made *LIFE*. A Ferguson-designed, wall-less corn-processing plant was spectacular enough to merit three pages in *LIFE* in 1949. My placement "philosophy" was to aim for high-impact "hits" in publications that impressed my client's customers, a strategy I continue to believe in. That early experience forever made me respectful of those who make blockbuster placements in major media.

In 1951, Elias (Buck) Buchwald, who remained with Burson-Marsteller for the next fifty years, joined me as Roy Heatly's replacement. Although Roy had the potential for a promising career in public relations, he wanted to live in California and work in television news. He became West Coast manager of CBS News at an early age before moving on to San Francisco's KRON-TV as news director. In his later years, he returned to public relations by establishing a firm in Sacramento that was acquired by a Burson-Marsteller competitor.

As I have frequently said, Buck played a seminal role in evolving the Burson-Marsteller culture and methodology, and in making us the world's largest public relations firm thirty-three years later. In fairness, I must credit my wife, Bette, for identifying Buck as a potential professional colleague. Buck worked for a medium-sized public relations firm that had the magnesium insulation industry account. In her role as secretary/office manager, Bette came to know Buck during our month-long collaboration on a trade magazine article, and she arranged for us to have lunch. He was exactly the person I was looking for, a graduate engineer who could write, with several years experience at a successful public relations firm. His salary was $5,600 a year and I offered him $6,500. He accepted on the spot.

Buck reinforced my small firm's ability to service business-to-business clients whose products and processes required technical understanding. (We were among the original high techies!) We had superb relationships with business and trade press editors who welcomed articles featuring our clients, and almost without exception, clients valued our services. But while some clients increased fees at the start of a new year, new business was elusive. We got too few "times at bat" – too few opportunities to demonstrate our capabilities. And we found it especially difficult to penetrate the larger blue chip companies we so desperately wanted on our client list.

A half century later, I still remember our disappointment after learning we had not won an account for which we felt highly qualified and had invested many hours preparing a proposal. It was the Grinding Wheel Institute, a group of grinding wheel manufacturers whose product was used primarily to sharpen tools. The market was static and industry leaders wanted to promote grinding wheels as a production tool to remove rough edges and create smooth surfaces. The annual fee was $50,000 – a "plum" account for a small firm like ours. The selection committee seemed to agree with our approach, and the "chemistry" during the question-answer period gave us confidence we had won the business. Several days later, we were told another firm was selected. We later learned the committee felt we "lacked depth and back-up staff" to service the account. Buck and I were so disappointed that in later years we often used "Grinding Wheel Institute" as code whenever we felt overly confident after a new business presentation.

Another incident from that period I will always remember followed the birth of our first son, Scott, on May 28, 1952. Mother and child were scheduled to leave the hospital at noon on June 3, which coincided with the final luncheon of the annual conference of my client, the American Institute of Architects. The world famous architect Frank Lloyd Wright was the speaker and press interest was high since it was Wright's first New York appearance in many years. Without sharing my dilemma with my client, I considered my presence at the luncheon absolutely essential on so auspicious an occasion. I informed my wife, Bette, that I had arranged for my closest friend – a Southerner with whom I was in college at Ole Miss and well-known to Bette – to escort her and our son from French Hospital to our apartment at 223 East 61st Street. The immediate repercussions were nothing compared to those that have persisted over the past half-century. Even now, whenever my wife has reason to question my regard and attentiveness, she is prone to remind me that I failed to bring her home from the hospital with our firstborn child. But no one could ever question my commitment to clients!

Many, if not most, entrepreneurs delight in telling "horror" stories centered on their inability to come up with the rent or meet the payroll. Though I had capi tal of only $3,000 when I launched my business, I never experienced a month when I lacked cash in the bank to meet the payroll and pay the bills. My secret was, simply, that most of my clients paid their monthly fees in advance. Large out-of-pocket expenses – such as printing or paid advertising – was also paid, at least in part, in advance of my getting billed by the supplier or publisher.

One nerve-wracking experience came in 1950 when my first and largest client Ferguson, was acquired by the Morrison-Knudsen Company, a big construction company based in Boise, Idaho. It had its own internal public relations depart ment and I was concerned that it would take over the work I had been doing My fears were dispelled when I presented results of the past five years to the new owners. Their reaction was that I had done a better job for Ferguson than their own people had done for M-K, a much larger company whose specialty was building highways, dams, airports, port facilities and other civil engineering proj ects. A few months later, three of Ferguson's senior executives, including the CEO, who had actually put me in business, decided to join forces with a small er New York firm called Walter Kidde Constructors. Their objective was to make Kidde a major player in the industrial engineer-builder category and an aggres sive publicity program was a major component of their business plan. My mis givings about dropping Ferguson as a client were tempered by the uncertaintie attendant to working with new owners, and I agreed to follow my friends to Kidde. My $1,000/month fee was increased to $1,250 and within a year, Kidde had more mentions in the business and trade press than any other engineering/construction firm.

───────── ◦◦◦◦ ─────────

Deciding how much to charge clients in those days was more an art than a sci ence. Immediately after the end of World War II, an account that generated annual revenues of $25,000 was well worth having. Hill & Knowlton, even then an industry leader, was widely known to require a "minimum" annual fee of $36,000 and Carl Byoir & Associates, then the largest public relations firm charged $50,000/year for corporate clients and $60,000 for trade associations Smaller firms charged what the traffic would bear, usually ranging upward of $500 a month. Nowadays, those numbers seem trifling – but that was hardly the case more than half a century ago before the onset of inflation. In those days, an acceptable starting salary in public relations was $75 a week or about $4,000 a year. A mid-level account executive was paid in the $6,000/$8,000 range. Anyone making a thousand dollars a month was considered an executive. It is also informative to remember that in the late 1940s a subway ride cost five cents; the meter "throw" on a taxi was twenty cents; *The New York Times* cost five cents and the *New York Daily News* three cents; an orchestra seat to a Broadway show was $4.80 and a single room at the Waldorf Astoria was $10/$12. In terms of purchasing power, the $25,000 budget of that era equated to $200/$250,000 in the early years of the 21st century.

Although public relations firms in that era did not bill by the hour, hourly rates would have been proportionate to the salary. For example, using a three or even four times salary multiple to cover overhead and profit, the billing rate for a mid-level account executive would be less than $20 an hour. The billing rate for an executive paid $20,000 would be in the $50 range. The first time I was called in for a crisis management assignment – it was a hostile corporate takeover and I was recruited by a major law firm. I was told by the attorney-in-charge that I should bill at the rate of $300 a day. The project lasted about three weeks and I regarded it as a windfall.

Since client cost accounting was yet to be applied in public relations firms (true also of advertising agencies of the day), I allocated my time in those early days instinctively – enough to produce sufficient results to keep the client happy and enough to do those things needed to make the business grow.

<hr />

Almost sixty years since I decided to start a public relations business, I have wondered retrospectively about my audacity, even recklessness, in presuming I had the competence and experience for such an enterprise. I had never set foot in a public relations firm and had met few public relations professionals. To be truthful, I equated publicity with public relations and regarded my scrapbook packed with articles about my employer as credential enough to convince prospective clients that I was an effective publicist. I used the term "public relations" to identify my business even though the service I offered was largely gaining editorial coverage in the media. The fact is, I thought public relations and publicity were synonymous and interchangeable!

In hindsight, I have tried to reconstruct how I came to learn that publicity is a subset of the more encompassing public relations. I have also tried to recon-

struct the evolutionary process that expanded my horizons from publicist to pub
lic relations counselor. In so doing, I have no intention of demeaning the worl
of the publicist or, as we describe them in today's patois, media relations special
ists. I think publicists are as critical to the public relations "process" as strategi
thinkers, and that truly creative media relations specialists are as rare as proactiv
strategic thinkers. Placing a story in a major publication was, for me, a thrillin;
experience and, on those infrequent occasions that I have done so in recent years
it still is.

My early knowledge of public relations came largely from reading the meage
supply of published materials of that era, and I recall two books in particular.

The first was written by the then-popular Washington pundit, Walte
Lippmann. Titled *Public Opinion* and published in 1922, it was intended t
educate elected officials on the need for an informed electorate in a democrati
society. It offered a methodology that elected officials could use to communicat
with constituents. Lippmann correctly foresaw the impact that two then-nev
inventions, radio and motion pictures, would have on forming attitudes an
creating expectations not only in this country but globally. I reread th
Lippmann book in the early days of the Internet and marveled at the juxtaposi
tion of the new technology with movies and radio in their ability to impact th
opinion-formation process.

The second was the classic, *Crystallizing Public Opinion* by Edward L. Bernay;
published in 1923, a book I believe should be mandatory reading for everyon
in public relations. Bernays, in effect, documented the methodology of practic
ing public relations. Written almost a century ago, it has as much validity toda
as when it first appeared. The first person to use the term "public relations coun
selor," Bernays painstakingly described how people process information to forn
the opinions and attitudes that influence their behavior. His basic thesis is tha
the mission of public relations is to impact public attitudes and opinion in orde
to motivate a specific behavior. He emphasized that public relations is a factor o
both behavior and communications – in short, doing good deeds and telling peo
ple what you've done or, put another way, behaving in a manner that accords wit
the public interest and effectively communicating your actions to parties at inter
est. And he encouraged the use of research to measure attitudes and opinion as
determinant of public relations goals and effectiveness.

In addition to reading about public relations, I sought out public relation
organizations that gave me access to others who shared my interests. In 1948,
joined a forerunner of the present Public Relations Society of America, th

National Association of Public Relations Counsel. I volunteered for committee work and began to meet other public relations practitioners – almost exclusively males because most females in public relations then worked in food, fashion and cosmetics. In 1949, I was a founding member of a small New York-based group called the Industrial Publicity Association. Our 25 members included representatives of business-to-business companies like General Electric, Union Carbide, Alcoa and U.S. Steel and four or five public relations firms that represented b-to-b, what we then termed "industrial," clients. At monthly meetings, a member presented an actual case history which we then discussed in detail. For me, it was both a learning experience and an opportunity to meet prospects and competitors. The organization existed for almost a quarter century.

Another group that I was asked to join in the mid-1950s called itself The Pride and Alarm Society ("we take pride in what we do, alarm at what we see"). Somewhat "elitist," its 16 to 18 members met monthly at the old Biltmore Hotel on the northeast corner of Madison and 43rd Street and represented a cross section of large, mid-size and small firms. Programs were unstructured discussions on the business of public relations plus a liberal quotient of news and gossip about colleagues. To some considerable extent, the justification of the organization was that it provided a reason for people who shared common interests and enjoyed one another's company to get together. For me, it was another source of information about both the business and practice of public relations – and it gave me access to senior public relations professionals I would otherwise have lacked.

Another organization I joined was the Overseas Press Club, a meeting place for reporters and editors. The club's dining room was for many years one of my favorite places for lunch and made a strong impression on most client guests.

Looking back, I believe my most valuable lessons came from the experience gained from responding to the myriad situations that affected my clients' business – in effect, the on-the-job training that is endemic in providing public relations services to clients with active businesses. As issues arose, clients usually called on me because such matters almost always had the potential to find their way into the media. One of the first issues I worked on was in the early days of nuclear power. As a contender to design and construct the first commercial nuclear power plants, my client was concerned that incipient anti-nuclear efforts would cause the deferral or cancellation of major contracts. I took a proactive role in organizing a pro-nuclear industry group called the American Nuclear Society (ANS). I wrote the announcement release in 1948 and ANS was my client until it merged with a new more broadly based organization several years later.

My involvement with the nuclear issue taught me some of the rudiments of wha we now call "issues management" and it also expanded my definition of public relations.

A year or so later I got more deeply involved in another "issue" assignment My client was the American Watch Assemblers Association, a group of compa nies that imported Swiss-made watch movements and put them in cases manu factured in the U.S. I was hired to provide media support for an initiative to defeat legislation that would impose a punitive tariff on Swiss-made watch move ments. After about six months, Congress did enact a tariff on imported 18-jewe watch movements, but it was a Pyrrhic victory for my client's competitors Thereafter Swiss manufacturers shipped movements with only 17 jewels and th 18th (whose utility I have always wondered about!) was put in place after arriva in the U.S. This was my first experience in a lobbying effort.

Chapter 3

Burson-Marsteller Origins: My First Meeting with Bill Marsteller

In late January 1952, sitting in my small office in the New York Daily News Building on East 42nd Street, I received a telephone call from a close friend at *The New York Times* that changed my life. Harry Leather sold industrial advertising for *The Times* and I had developed a close relationship with him because I wrote and placed Ferguson advertising. Harry called to alert me that he had recommended me to Bill Marsteller, the owner of an industrial advertising agency in Chicago and Pittsburgh. Marsteller had come to New York to identify a small public relations firm that could handle a project for his agency's largest client, Rockwell Manufacturing Company (now Rockwell International). The project was to publicize a helicopter purchased by Rockwell's chairman, W. F. (Al) Rockwell Jr. The news peg was that it would be the first helicopter used for executive travel. His reason for wanting a helicopter was to overcome his vice-presidents' resistance to visiting Rockwell plants within 150 miles of Pittsburgh. At the time, the interstate highway program was barely off the drawing boards and a two-hundred-mile trip over and around the hills of western Pennsylvania meant driving the better part of a day.

Eager to add a distinguished name to our client roster, I telephoned Bill

Marsteller to say that I would be in Chicago the following week. By coincidence, I had scheduled a visit to a Ferguson construction site on the outskirts of Chicago to do a case history. Marsteller appreciated my call and, impressed with the unqualified recommendation from my friend at *The New York Times*, said he looked forward to my visit. Later, I learned he had also spoken with a *New York Times* business news writer, Hartley Barclay, who was even more lavish in praising me. Through the years I have often wondered what would have happened to me and my business if I had not already planned a trip to Chicago just as Marsteller learned about me from my friends at *The New York Times*. Certainly, I would have telephoned him. Most probably, we would have agreed on a meeting at a convenient time. But most likely, he would have picked up the names of other publicists against whom I would have had to compete. Throughout our subsequent near-40 year association, Bill Marsteller told friends how impressed he was with me for "dropping everything and getting on a train to Chicago to make a new business call."

Marsteller and I were attuned to one another from the outset. Our lives had much in common – we were both writers, we were both editors of high school and college newspapers, we both paid our way through college by "stringing" for a daily newspaper, and we both shared an entrepreneurial bent. Bill outlined the assignment and was quick to admit that his advertising agency lacked the know-how needed to satisfy the client. I quickly assured him that I could get the job done. The next step was to visit the client in Pittsburgh.

Within minutes after being introduced to Al Rockwell, I realized that I had won the business. Marsteller was Al Rockwell's trusted confidant and it was obvious they had made their decision prior to my arrival in Pittsburgh. We agreed that my compensation would be on a per diem basis – $500 per day – largely because of the indefinite nature of the assignment. In fact, the helicopter manufacturer, Sikorsky (which some years later became a Burson-Marsteller client) had not yet committed to a delivery date. That, however, did not deter my getting started on my assignment. Al Rockwell wanted me to be well-grounded in his company before undertaking what I considered to be the real work of convincing editors that this was indeed a story worth publishing. He arranged for me to speak to a half dozen vice presidents and to visit several Rockwell plants within 150 miles of corporate headquarters. I also visited Sikorsky in Hartford as part of my indoctrination. While I learned a great deal about the company and about helicopters, most of what I learned was extraneous to the task at hand. But the income was good and I had the time. At the beginning of July, some three months into the project, Sikorsky informed Rockwell that delivery of the S-55 helicopter would be delayed a year because of the Korean War.

For me and my firm, it was both good news and it was bad news. The good news was that my day of reckoning was postponed – the more I knew Al Rockwell, the more certain I became that I could never reach his expectation level for news coverage of his new helicopter. Also, I began to appreciate Bill Marsteller's astuteness in walking away from the 'hot potato' that I had inherited. The bad news was, no work on the helicopter, no income.

However, my many talks with Rockwell executives paid dividends. I had learned that Rockwell's power tool division, Delta, was preparing to introduce what the company believed to be a "revolutionary" new combination power tool expected to take the home workshop market by storm. I suggested that my talents be diverted to publicizing the new power tool while awaiting the helicopter.

On this assignment, I actually exceeded my client's expectations. In a late November 1952 issue of *LIFE* magazine, then the nation's most potent advertising medium, an article about Rockwell's "new and revolutionary DeltaShop" filled three pages. Within ten days, DeltaShops were sold out. Rockwell's power tool plant worked overtime to accommodate the holiday demand. The folks at Rockwell thought I could walk on water. My strategy was to capitalize on my triumph by proposing that Rockwell become an ongoing retainer client. I took the overnight train to Pittsburgh for another visit with Al Rockwell, who had gathered his senior officers for a lunch celebrating the *LIFE* story. It's not surprising that the timing of my visit made my proposal an easy sell. When asked what I required as a monthly fee, I took a deep breath and asked for $3,000 a month and got it. Our largest account at the time paid a monthly fee of $1,250.

The Marsteller advertising agency's second largest client was Clark Equipment Company, the world's premier manufacturer of forklift trucks. For some time, Bill had urged me to meet Clark CEO George Spatta and a date was arranged just days after winning the Rockwell business. In the course of twenty-four hours, Clark also became a client and it happened in a most unusual way. Spatta, an engineer who grew up in New York's Hell's Kitchen, asked me for "a concrete example" of what public relations could do for his company. After a half hour conversation, I felt the best way to demonstrate the magic of public relations was to write and place an article on Clark/Spatta in one of the major New York newspapers.

In those days at year-end, newspaper business pages were chock full of industry roundups called "year-enders" that reviewed the financial and market prospects of an industry or a company. I treated my talk with Spatta as an interview on the outlook for the materials handling business in the new year and specifically, his projections for the company he headed, Clark Equipment. I returned to my office to write the story and later rejoined him to get his approval for the comments that I had attributed to him. Meanwhile, I telephoned a close friend, a business reporter for the *New York Herald-Tribune*, to alert him to a story that I thought would be of interest and that it would be in his hands well before his deadline.

The next morning the Clark materials-handling story prominently quoting George Spatta was on the *Herald-Trib*'s first business page with nary a word changed, except for the reporter's byline. My telephone rang shortly before noon. "Spatta here," the voice said, "can you join me for lunch at the Biltmore in thirty minutes?" His first words on my arrival were, "Now I know what public relations is." He then told me he had spent the morning at the Morgan Guaranty Bank renegotiating his company's credit line. The bankers greeted him with "Great story, George" and congratulated him on the favorable outlook for the materials handling business in 1953. "I got the loan for a quarter of a point less than I expected to pay," he told me. "That's what I call good public relations." Our talk then turned to structuring an ongoing relationship and I left the lunch with a $4,000/month commitment.

Having added the Rockwell and Clark business in the space of two weeks, more than sixty percent of my firm's business consisted of the two Marsteller referrals. Though Bill and I had communicated regularly for ten months, we had never discussed either a formal working relationship or any financial reward for his referrals. I thought the time had arrived for us to talk about a more formal association. We agreed to meet for breakfast in the Edwardian Room at New York's Plaza Hotel the first Saturday in the new year.

Overlooking a snow-covered Central Park on a cold sun-lit day, I proposed forming a new company that would be free-standing and jointly owned in approximately equal shares by me and the Marsteller agency. Bill Marsteller, a former news reporter, appreciated my strongly held view that a public relations business should not be subordinated as a department or division of an advertising agency. The vision I articulated called for an enterprise that would operate to the same high professional standards as the most respected independently-owned public relations firms. Clearly, I wanted our new firm to be measured against the top public relations firms rather than as an adjunct advertising agency service. To be candid, my model was Hill & Knowlton, then the world's largest and most respected public relations firm. I got no disagreement from Bill.

Actually, the only subject at issue was who would own fifty-one percent majority control. I, of course, proposed that I hold the controlling interest since I would be responsible for building the business and doing the work, but Marsteller was adamant that his advertising agency should be the majority stockholder. In the years that followed, a legend has developed that by acceding to Marsteller's wish on the majority control issue, I got my name in front of the hyphen. Actually, there was never a question about whose name would go first.

Bill Marsteller went into the advertising agency business in May 1951 after resigning as vice-president-marketing at Rockwell Manufacturing Company. Bill joined Rockwell in 1947 when Rockwell acquired Edward Valves, East Chicago, Ind., where he was in charge of advertising. He commuted to Rockwell's corporate office and had no intention of relocating his family to Pittsburgh. In 1950, Rockwell decided it had outgrown its two principal advertising agencies, one in Chicago headed by Ernest Gebhardt, the other in Pittsburgh by Rod Reed. Bill's boss (and the largest client of both agencies) Al Rockwell, proposed that the two agencies join forces under Bill Marsteller's management. In effect, Bill bought the two businesses and Marsteller Gebhardt & Reed came into being by changing the names on the doors of the two agencies. Bill remained in Chicago and was joined by Richard C. (Dick) Christian, a young market researcher at Rockwell who succeeded him as CEO when he retired in 1979.

About a year after Burson-Marsteller began operations, my recommendation that Marsteller Gebhardt & Reed establish a New York presence was embraced by the MGR board. I believed New York represented an opportunity to expand Marsteller's advertising business and, at the same time, provide prospects for public relations services. Bill asked me to take responsibility for getting the agency started in New York and we agreed that an acquisition would hasten the process.

In December 1954, we signed an agreement to acquire Rickard & Company. Started post-World War I, Rickard was once the largest industrial agency but never fully recovered from the Great Depression. Its three owners, proteges of the deceased founder, neared retirement and were ripe for a proposition that fulfilled their joint objective of "cashing them out" and protecting the jobs of their 30 colleagues. On January 1, 1955, Marsteller Rickard Gebhardt & Reed became the new name. Five years later, the New York office was on the way to becoming Marsteller Advertising's largest office and Bill and his family moved to New York.

In 1973, following the deaths of "Geb" Gebhardt and Rod Reed and recogniz
ing that the agency was commonly referred to as "Marsteller," the name wa
changed to Marsteller Inc.

Chapter 4

❦

Burson-Marsteller, The First Decade:
Rockwell and Clark, The Seeds of Success

When Burson-Marsteller opened for business on March 2, 1953, with a staff of five in the New York Daily News Building at 220 East 42nd Street, it was, to the outside world, an event of little significance. No one could, or would even have dared, predict that the new enterprise would one day have major influence on the business of public relations. Bill Marsteller's observation that our union with his advertising agency – then called Marsteller Gebhardt & Reed – would enable us to deliver a "total communications" service to clients and prospects went largely unnoticed. Thirty years later "integrated communications" entered the marketing lexicon as a recent discovery.

Like our advertising siblings, the new Burson-Marsteller positioned itself as a specialist firm serving the industrial market. Our two largest clients, Rockwell Manufacturing Company and Clark Equipment Company – each obtained only three months earlier – represented two-thirds of our total income. Among the early conglomerates, Rockwell produced valves for the petroleum and power industries, gas and water meters, home workshop and light industrial power tools and taxi meters. Clark, the world's largest manufacturer of forklift trucks, also made heavy-duty automotive power trains – transmissions, axles, axle housing for trucks and off-highway equipment. The first publicly-owned companies ever worked for, Clark was listed on the New York Stock Exchange, and Rockwell shares traded on the Over-the-Counter market (forerunner to today's NAS DAQ). When the first *FORTUNE* 500 listing appeared in 1955, Clark was 314th with sales of $91 million and Rockwell was 354th with sales of $77 million. Although the numbers would be about seven times larger in today's dollars in my world they were really big companies; in actuality, they were in the mid size range of American corporations.

Rockwell and Clark were, to be candid, training grounds where my young associates and I learned how to work with clients requiring a broad range of public relations services. In reality, neither was a single client. Rather, Rockwell was six clients with six budgets: corporate/financial, Nordstrom valves (petroleum and natural gas), Delta power tools, gas meters and regulators, water meters and Edward valves (power generation). Over the years, our original $3,000/month corporate-wide budget estimate grew more than ten-fold as we developed programs to support marketing initiatives to specific buyer audiences. I had never worked for a client whose needs were on so large a scale and neither had my associate Buck Buchwald.

Colonel Willard F. Rockwell created his company after World War I by combining a water meter manufacturer with a firm that produced gas meters and called it Pittsburgh Equitable Meter Company. The firm grew mainly by acquisition. In the early 1950s, its name was changed to Rockwell Manufacturing Company and the founder appointed his 39-year-old son, a Pennsylvania State University-educated engineer known as "Al," chief operating officer and CEO heir-apparent.

Bill Marsteller, who had been Rockwell's chief marketing officer before going into the advertising agency business, spearheaded the name change initiative. To make Al Rockwell more visible in the business community, Marsteller created "Rockwell Report," a series of monthly advertisements that ran for a quarter century in *Time*, *Newsweek*, *The Wall Street Journal* and *BusinessWeek*. The ad format resembled a newspaper column – the heading a small photo of Al Rockwell alongside "Rockwell Report." A typical ad contained a lead "commentary" item reflecting the company's "related diversification" philosophy followed by news items about Rockwell products. Magazine ads were two-thirds of a page and newspaper ads were two columns ten inches deep. Research showed that "Rockwell Report" was the best read ad month after month among business readers. The corporate public relations program we developed focused on "related diversification" as the Rockwell differentiator.

For the Rockwell account, I took responsibility for corporate/financial and Buck Buchwald headed marketing/product publicity. It was, of course, immediately apparent that we would require additional people to service the business. While Rockwell management mostly was in Pittsburgh, Delta power tools – the business unit with the largest budget – was in Milwaukee. Early on Bill and I decided to open a Chicago office as soon as we could hire a manager. Delta power tools and the Clark business units would be its first clients. Since Rockwell did not have a public relations executive on staff, we decided with our client to station a full-time Burson-Marsteller employee at Rockwell corporate headquarters. That arrangement worked well until 1957 when Rockwell hired a full-time public relations director and we opened a Pittsburgh office.

A *Pittsburgh Press* feature writer, George Thomas, became our interface with Rockwell. He coordinated our activities at Rockwell, covered Rockwell business units for news and wrote speeches and by-lined articles for senior managers. Our close relationship made us privy to management reports and other confidential information. For many years, Bill Marsteller and I attended Rockwell's annual three-day management meeting where plans and goals were presented by business units. For me it was not only an opportunity to know our client but also to learn firsthand how a successful business was managed.

George Thomas was among the first of a long list of colorful characters at Burson-Marsteller. His achievements included establishing the George Thomas Clubs of America whose chapters consisted exclusively of people named George Thomas. The idea came to him when he couldn't remember his home telephone number and discovered about twenty-five other George Thomas listings in the Pittsburgh directory (he remembered his street address). He sent postcards inviting each George Thomas to a Dutch treat lunch. Most showed up, they decided to meet at regular intervals and he repeated the process in several other cities. About 1965, he returned to *The Pittsburgh Press* where he resumed writing feature stories until his retirement to Florida.

Rockwell was transformed into a much larger company during the 1970s and 1980s. After acquiring North American Aviation, it changed its name to Rockwell International, moved corporate headquarters to California and became a major factor in aerospace and electronics. It built the B-1 bomber, the space vehicle that put the first men on the moon and the space shuttle. As new generations of management took over at Rockwell, our relationship with the company began to wither after being their sole public relations firm for more than thirty years. By the early 1990s, they were no longer a client, having taken most of the public relations function in-house. In recent years Rockwell became a much smaller company after selling its aerospace business to Boeing, spinning off Collins avionics and its electronics business, and selling all the b-to-b Pittsburgh business units. Today Rockwell Automation is a one-business company that designs, manufactures and installs automated production lines. I am certain that Colonel Rockwell and his son Al, who were so acquisitive by nature, would be less than pleased that what they created has been so dismantled. (For a decade following World War II, Colonel Rockwell was non-executive chairman of three publicly-listed companies.)

Clark Equipment at the outset was essentially three accounts: corporate/ financial, materials handling industrial trucks and automotive components. Like Rockwell, it had no public relations function either at corporate or at its forklift truck unit. As with Rockwell, Buck took responsibility for product publicity, although the day-to-day work was handled in our new Chicago office. On corporate/financial, I reported directly to the CEO, George Spatta.

My working relationship with Spatta was among the closest of my entire career. During the dozen years he was CEO and for five years more as a board member, we met almost every other week. We often traveled together when he addressed financial analysts and other business groups or visited Clark facilities. Since he expected me to be fully aware of developments in Clark's business, I also met regularly with the chief financial officer, general counsel and business unit managers. For someone who once had difficulty understanding what public relations could do for his company, George Spatta was a quick learner. A couple years after we started working together, *The New York Times* published a flattering article about him and his company. Over lunch a few days later he started our conversation with "you public relations guys are a lot like dope pushers." Noting my perplexed reaction, he continued "you public relations guys get people like me hooked by getting our names in the paper and the time soon comes when we start liking it." I took his remark as a compliment.

My role at Clark was often somewhat beyond the normal scope of public relations services. During the two years he was selecting his successor, he asked me to be both his "eyes and ears" and his sounding board. In all candor, my role was largely listening as he recited, time and again, positives and negatives applying to the four executives he had identified as contenders. My relationship with Spatta was known to each of the four, but, miraculously, none ever asked me to violate the confidences which had been entrusted to me. Even more startling, I was able to maintain friendly relationships with those under review (two of them, business unit heads, controlled more than half our budget!). The person he selected, considered the least favored contender early in the process, was my choice (unvoiced) from the beginning.

For me he was a great teacher and mentor. He would pose such questions as "do you know the difference between FIFO and LIFO (first in/first out and last in/first out – two methods for valuing inventories). When I confessed knowing only what the initials stood for, he launched into a 30-minute discussion on the criteria for selecting one over the other. Another time, he spoke on methods to motivate senior executives and defended Clark's compensation practice – low fixed salaries and outrageously high bonuses (for that era). In fact, *Forbes* magazine in the 1960s cited Clark as one of the country's highest paying corporations. Spatta's compensation package for the previous year was over $400,000 and his direct reports each earned more than $300,000 – a lot of money in those days. His comment: "We always take care of our stockholders first with a good dividend – management deserves its fair share of what's left over."

Frustrated because Clark was unknown and, in his view, its shares undervalued, Spatta specifically wanted to increase the company's visibility and gain greater understanding of the company's potential among financial analysts. At that time financial public relations was in its infancy – in fact, the financial analyst function was itself relatively new. By getting acquainted with several "security analysts" (as they were then called), I learned that they yearned for information from companies in the categories they followed. Also, I learned that security analyst societies and "splinter groups" (those who specialized by industry) welcomed CEOs as speakers at their meetings in New York and regional financial centers like Boston, Chicago and San Francisco. I proposed that Spatta commit to personal visits with eight to ten influential analysts and speeches to each of the financial analyst societies. He quickly embraced my proposal and made the further comment "let them know I will take their telephone calls" – an offer that made him unique among CEOs and popular with the financial analyst community. We also launched a quarterly "Clark Financial News Letter" for security analysts and financial writers. Its purpose was to "explain the numbers" and provide insights on trends affecting the company's businesses. At the time, Clark was recognized as a frontrunner in disclosure – in today's verbiage, "transparency." One result was that Clark was frequently cited as "a junior blue chip" – a result not only of open communication but also of consistent sales and earnings growth and a secure meaningful dividend.

Spatta's greatest achievement was making Clark a major factor in the then-crowded and highly competitive construction machinery business by introducing a line of tractor shovels whose advanced design outflanked the industry. Our press launch for the new product in May 1954 was akin to a car manufacturers annual new model introduction. It positioned Clark as a significant player in construction machinery. Staged at a working construction site, reporters/editors were encouraged to take the wheel of the new easy-to-operate earthmoving machines. They actually dug and moved dirt! Our principal message was that the new "Michigan" line started with "a blank sheet of drawing paper" – the only line of construction machinery designed from "scratch" without regard to protecting existing tooling or parts inventories. Our efforts produced enthusiastic coverage in construction and materials handling media. Almost overnight the "Michigan" brand was second only to Caterpillar. Five years later the industry's leading magazine, *Engineering News-Record*, published a lengthy cover story titled "The Solid Gold Tractor Shovel" – a detailed account of Clark's rapid rise in the industry.

Clark tractor shovels outsold Caterpillar for some 20 years. For all that time, we supported the marketing program with steady case history coverage in national, regional and local media – frequently cover stories with prominent display of the "Michigan" brand name. Most gratifying to me and my associates who worked on Clark's Construction Machinery Division – among them John La Sage (who claims to have done 225 case histories), Lew Keim and John Murphy – were the recognition and support we got from our client, starting with Clarence Killebrew, who headed the "Michigan" business unit, and CMD's long-time advertising director, Colin Kennedy. Our joint effort was a model for future client/agency partnerships.

Our relationship with Clark continued for 45 years until the company was the object of a hostile takeover by Ingersoll-Rand in 1998. We had worked with five CEOs. For 35 of those years Louis J. Behre, who joined Clark as George Spatta's assistant about the time we were first hired, was our principal contact. Joanne Tremulis, a managing director at B-M/Chicago, succeeded me as principal interface on the corporate business and John La Sage, our long-time senior officer in the Midwest, supervised our work for Clark business units. As CEO Leo McKernan said at a dinner in 1993 marking our 40th anniversary as Clark's sole public relations firm, "you guys at Burson-Marsteller were members of the Clark family long before I came on board."

Our relationship with Rockwell and Clark led us to establish our first office outside the U.S. when they, coincidentally, in 1960, established Canadian subsidiaries. Though we knew their budgets would fall far short of assuring us a breakeven operation, we opened an office in Toronto, the first U.S. public relations firm to do so. While it would be twenty years before the operation grew significantly, we attracted a lot of early attention in Canada. Our first general manager, Bill Dulmage, was one of Canada's best-known World War II heroes. As squadron leader of a Mosquito fighter group that carried out a daring low-level bombing mission on a German ammunition train in Holland, Dulmage received Canada's highest military decoration and was the aviator prototype of a popular cartoon strip. Unfortunately, he died of cancer five years after joining us.

The influence of Rockwell and Clark on me personally and on Burson-Marsteller institutionally would be hard to overstate. The knowledge gained from them on how publicly-owned corporations did business was deep and diverse. Both successful and, even in retrospect, I believe well-managed, the two companies differed greatly. Rockwell was the prototype of a buttoned-down Harvard Business School case history on how a company should be managed. It had a structured management hierarchy, written policy guidelines and a well-planned aggressive acquisition program. Clark management was intuitive and opportunistic, its two end-product business units almost totally independent of one another. As a CEO, Al Rockwell managed by consensus. George Spatta believed "a bit of tension" among senior officers produced a more competitive environment and he used a "carrot and stick" technique to motivate his business unit managers and senior reports. Spatta was fond of saying "my guys know that if they deliver the bottom line, I'll make them rich." It worked. For 25 years post-World War II, Clark was among the two or three top gainers in share price on the New York Stock Exchange.

Though not unusual in that era for mid-sized industrial companies, neither

Rockwell nor Clark had an in-house public relations officer when we started working for them. It was both a blessing and a burden. It gave my associates and me considerable freedom to mix freely with management, to learn their business, and to propose and implement innovative – sometimes risky – initiatives. The other side of the coin was that it was easy for the client to pinpoint responsibility – if ever we failed to deliver on our promise, there was no place to hide, no one to defend us. The fact that both companies were clients for more than four decades – even after they each had public relations officers on staff – attests to our performance. They got their money's worth and a generation of my colleagues got a lot of learning that would serve them well with future clients. In both cases, however, we recommended that they have in-house public relations executives.

As the decade of the 1950s came to an end, Burson-Marsteller had 25 clients and revenues of half a million dollars (almost four million in today's dollars). Our most notable account win – in 1956 – was the Electro-Motive Division of General Motors, the non-automotive division that manufactures diesel locomotives. Burson-Marsteller was the only public relations firm employed by General Motors and winning that business had an enormous impact on our future. Another significant addition was Universal Oil Products Company, the developer of the catalytic cracking process for making gasoline. Also on our expanding client list were the country's largest nuts and bolt company, the largest producer of chromium plating materials, a machine tool manufacturer, the premier maker of milking machines, the largest maker of coke and coal-tar derivatives, the largest distributor of rail and steel sheet piling and a pipeline company – all "industrial" clients with the exception of Rockwell's Delta power tool division whose market was home workshop hobbyists and the now-forgotten Gibson Refrigerator, then a division of Hupp Corporation, the maker of the once-fabled Huppmobile.

Toward the end of the 1950s, my associates and I recognized that the business model that was working so well for us – restricting ourselves to industrial clients – would soon seriously limit our growth. On several occasions, we were unable to take on a new client because of a conflict with an existing client. The more successful we became in our "niche," the more difficult it was to grow. In 1959, we engaged this issue in a weekend "long-range planning" meeting to discuss our future.

Bill Marsteller wisely enlisted a facilitator, Dr. Melvin Anshen of Columbia University's Graduate School of Business, to chair the meeting. Participants included Marsteller, Buchwald, Richard C. (Dick) Christian, who some years later succeeded Bill as CEO of Marsteller advertising agency, and a few additional senior officers representing both public relations and advertising. Before the meeting, we hired an independent research firm to survey industrial companies to determine how we fared against our competition in awareness and reputation. This research confirmed that clients and prospects preferred Marsteller Advertising and Burson-Marsteller over our competitors by a wide margin.

Our long-range planning agenda was designed to answer such issues as "the kind of public relations firm we want to be in ten to twenty years;" "the profile of our 'model' future client;" and "the steps we must take to move from our present position to our desired position a decade or two hence." After a full day of free-ranging, largely unfocused discussion, we finally got on track by defining the kind of clients we hoped to attract in future years. Simply stated, our objective was to merit a client list consisting of large publicly owned multinational corporations requiring a broad range of public relations, public affairs and communications services in the developed countries around the world. Having made that determination, it was relatively easy to identify what we needed to do to equip ourselves to accomplish our goal. We put together an inventory of existing attributes and assets and listed the specialties and facilities needed to give us the capability to achieve our objective.

Our "to do" list included:

- Establish a consumer marketing capability.
- Establish a Washington (public affairs) capability.
- Establish a West Coast presence.
- Establish an international presence – in Europe, Asia, Latin America and Australia.
- Strengthen our corporate/investor relations capability.
- Install an effective personnel evaluation system; install financial controls and do a better job of budgeting.
- Make the firm better known among companies we wanted as future clients (more effective publicity/marketing).
- Undertake a more aggressive recruiting program and provide a formal training program.

There was also a "soft" side of the agenda. We wanted to attract and retain the best people in the business. We wanted our reputation to be the most professional, most creative, most dependable, most highly regarded public relations firm in the world – recognized by the best people as the best place to work. We knew that would not happen unless we made it happen. While we never used the term, we talked about creating and nurturing a working environment that had Camelot-like qualities. I believe, as the years went by, we came as close as any firm in our business to realizing that impossible dream.

We left the meeting with a document we called a "long-range plan" – what today would be called a "strategic plan." We were energized to tackle our "to do" list and established a timetable against which to measure progress.

Rockwell and Clark put us on a trajectory that led to what I have often referred to as "our most significant defining moment." The starting point was the Treaty of Rome, an agreement that created the European Common Market effective 1958. Six nations with a population of 200 million committed themselves to remove all tariff barriers and trade restrictions and form a market that would be second in size and wealth only to the United States. While making my rounds at Rockwell and Clark, a subject of increasing resonance was when, where and how they would establish their presence in "the Common Market." Whether they should or would do so, I quickly learned, was never an issue.

The idea of taking Burson-Marsteller and Marsteller Advertising to Europe was quick in coming to me after learning of the stirrings in Europe to establish a continent-wide market. My own comfort level with Europe came naturally: I had spent almost two years there and my parents had emigrated from Europe to the U.S. Fifteen years after the end of World War II, I was well aware of its economic potential. On the basis of information at hand – particularly knowing that our clients were taking the new market seriously – it seemed a propitious time to establish a European advertising and public relations capability with our special credentials to serve industrial clients – much as we had done in the U.S. I was under no delusion that Rockwell and Clark income would underwrite a significant fraction of the cost of an overseas outpost. Rather, the main attraction to me was the opportunity to snare clients of U.S. origin who were not now U.S. clients but who later might join our U.S. roster. Also, I believed that industrial clients like ours would be the first U.S. companies to establish themselves in the new

European Common Market. As 1959 drew to an end, Bill Marsteller, still a self-styled midwestern isolationist (in just a few years he would embrace Europe with a fury!), agreed that Europe was an opportunity too good to ignore. We were on our way to becoming "international."

Chapter 5

⨺

Our Most Significant Defining Moment:
Establishing Burson-Marsteller in Europe

In November 1959 when we decided to go to Europe, Burson-Marsteller had three offices in the U.S. and was committed to open a fourth in Toronto. We had 50 employees, about half of them in New York, the remainder in Chicago and Pittsburgh. We were five years away from delivery of our first computer, an IBM 360, to do our bookkeeping, client billing and quarterly client P&L statements. Word processing was a decade away and, like our clients, we relied on the telephone and a wired typewriter called a "Telex" (maximum speed: 66 words per minute) for overseas communications. FAX (facsimile transmission) was still aborning. In reality, there were then few truly international brands – products sold and manufactured globally – IBM, Coca-Cola, Pan Am Airways and the grandfather of all global brands, Singer, the once ubiquitous sewing machine whose name has now all but disappeared from the business lexicon. And Mercedes-Benz and Rolls Royce and not many others.

News articles reporting American company plans to establish or expand operations in Europe reassured me that we were on the right course. To be totally candid, I never stopped to think of the financial risk we were taking, and Bill Marsteller never raised the issue. But over the past forty years, I have often asked myself whether I would have made the same decision had I known then what I later learned about risk-taking. The fact is, as of December 31, 1960, the combined net worth of Marsteller Advertising and Burson-Marsteller was about a million dollars. While I recognized that a new European enterprise must generate earnings quickly, it was three years before we broke even and five years before we earned a respectable profit. But my belief never wavered that companies with established agency relationships in the U.S. would be fair game in Europe. I felt strongly that they would recognize their need to identify themselves to buyers in countries where they were virtually unknown. Also, I envisioned a time when German companies would want to be better known in France and British companies would want to be better known on the Continent and vice versa.

Assisted by Jere Patterson, a consultant who brokered relationships for advertising agencies seeking international ties, I made three trips to Europe in 1960, each of two to three weeks duration, to explore how and where to establish our first office. A flight to London then entailed 16 hours in a piston-engine DC-6 and usually included a refueling stop in Gander, Newfoundland or Goose Bay, Labrador, and, on return flights, a mandatory stop in Shannon, Ireland, which boasted a humongous duty-free store.

U.S. corporations, I soon learned, favored Switzerland as a headquarters location because of the favorable Swiss tax rate. Since overseas subsidiaries of U.S. corporations were taxed at the rate of the country of domicile, the lower the local tax rate, the more favorable for the American company. Switzerland's tax rate was about thirty percent when it was fifty-two percent in the U.S. and even higher in some European countries. My objective was to establish both Burson-Marsteller public relations and Marsteller advertising offices that could offer industrial clients a total communications service. Following our U.S. example, the two businesses would maintain separate identities and each would seek its own clients. Until 1979, when we joined forces with Young & Rubicam, both public relations and Marsteller overseas advertising operations reported to me.

Geneva was my choice over Zurich simply because there was less local competition. Already a magnet for American corporations, Geneva was yet undiscovered by advertising and public relations firms while Zurich had several Swiss agencies with strong credentials. Another reason favoring Geneva was that it would be easier to obtain work permits for non-Swiss employees. Since local competitors had a voice in granting work permits, gaining approval was more likely than in Zurich. In fact, the largest Zurich advertising agency, the Rudolf Farner firm, actively supported our application for work permits given our agreement to stay in Geneva. Jere Patterson introduced me to Rudolf Farner, the most prominent person in Swiss advertising, and we maintained a friendly relationship until his death some twenty years later.

Our first overseas office opened for business in February 1961 when Robert (Bob) March, his spouse and their cat (additional air transportation cost from New York: $25) arrived in Geneva. March, in his mid-forties, was a Marsteller advertising account executive. He had two capabilities that made him my choice to manage our first overseas office: first, he was versatile – an excellent writer, a competent account manager, creative, good at new business, an energetic self-starter; second, he spoke French fluently (at the time one of the few in our company who could).

We did not have a single retainer client when we opened for business in Geneva. We landed our first within sixty days, a now nonexistent company called U.S. Industrial Chemicals (USIC), a division of National Distillers, which agreed to an annual retainer fee of $12,000 plus additional income for projects. Our initial assignment turned out to be a blockbuster. USIC wanted to make a major splash at Kunstoffe, the plastic industry's biggest trade show in Dusseldorf. But USIC started so late it couldn't get enough space. Our small staff in Geneva came up with the idea of renting an ocean-going boat that would both house their exhibit as well as customers and staff. It was docked on the Rhine, adjacent to the exhibit hall and was the hit of the show. To demonstrate the versatility of USIC plastics, we suggested creating oversized chess pieces that could be used to play what we named "deck chess." We had our first happy client in Europe and deck chess is now a part of ocean-going culture.

Total income the first year was about $100,000. With new business from Dow Chemical and IBM, Geneva revenues reached $400,000 in 1966 (about $2 million in 2003 dollars), and the office had its first profitable year. We had invested a half a million dollars, today a piddling amount for a company our size but then almost twenty percent of our net worth. Geneva subsequently became one of our most profitable offices, accounting for twenty-five percent of our combined net worth when we sold our business to Young & Rubicam in 1979.

In making my early rounds, I learned quickly that all of Europe could not be served from a single location. Rather, U.S. multinational clients required on-site representation in the larger markets like the United Kingdom, Germany, France and Italy. Brussels, having been designated European Common Market head-quarters, was correctly perceived to be the future principal European center for public affairs matters, thus making it an almost mandatory place to locate an office. Later, we knew we would also need our own offices in Spain, Holland and the Scandinavian countries. But I never imagined that one day we would have offices in Russia and the other Iron Curtain countries!

Lacking capital as well as people experienced in doing business in Europe, our initial strategy to service clients in the larger European markets was to acquire minority interests in industrial advertising agencies. This seemed preferable to linking ourselves to the relatively few public relations firms then operating on the Continent (London, however, was an exception; even then it was well populated with first-rate public relations firms). We negotiated ten to fifteen percent own-ership interests in five industrial (business-to-business) agencies: Roles & Parker Ltd. (London); Herman Bruder GmbH (Stuttgart); Sodipa S.A. (Paris); Cappellini S.r.l. (Italy); and Boden & Dechy S.A. (Brussels). None had a public relations capability, but they gave us access to the local business and trade press at a time when our business was mainly media relations. It didn't take long for us to learn that our strategy was faulted. In every country, with the exception of Germany (we subsequently bought the Bruder agency), we differed markedly in approach and methodology in the way we served clients. But the experience gave us the know-how and the confidence to launch our own offices. And attending board meetings in five countries provided me a crash course in the idiosyncratic nature of each of the national economies.

The Tax Reform Act of 1964 changed the landscape for locating overseas headquarters of U.S. companies and accelerated our expansion plans. This legis-lation negated tax havens like Switzerland by leveling the tax playing field. The impact on our small but growing European business was enormous. Many U.S.-owned Swiss-based subsidiaries, including half our clients, moved to Brussels. The urgent need for a Burson-Marsteller office in Belgium was therefore a "no brainer." To make the decision easier, the joint venture with our Belgian partner was faltering. They were as eager to repurchase their shares and be rid of us as we were to sell. Our contracts with European partners provided for share repurchase by the majority owner, and we ended the relationship with a modest profit on our small investment. The greatest return from holding minority positions in these European businesses was learning that business in Europe differed not only from the U.S. but also from one country to another.

Geneva started as a "bootstrap" operation. We added staff only after we got new clients or additional business from existing clients. Claude Marshall, a graduate ceramics engineer, was hired in New York in 1962 and dispatched to B-M/Geneva in early 1963. He remained as Geneva general manager and European general manager for more than thirty years. Peter Hynes, a B-M/ New York account executive, soon followed. Peter Walford, later to head B-M operations in Tokyo, Sydney and Canada, joined before the end of the decade. He had worked for the Australia-based Eric White consultancy's London office.

Knowing we could operate profitably in Europe, our confidence level was high when we entered Brussels. The original staff numbered fifteen, some hired in advance of need, and we leased enough space for at least thirty people. Four significant clients transferred from Geneva, including Texas Instruments and Parker Hannifin, and their account executives followed. While our expatriate employees preferred living in Geneva, Belgian work permits were easier to get and living costs were substantially lower.

The organizational structure in the two offices was similar. The general manager was an American with proven experience in our U.S. business. Group managers responsible for client relationships consisted of both Americans, mainly from within the company, and newly-hired U.K. professionals with either public relations or media experience. The nationality mix of expatriate professionals was about one-third American and two-thirds British, most of whom spoke French. The public relations talent pool was shallow on the Continent, but we worked hard identifying local nationals for entry-level and client-service positions. The support staff was almost totally local. Our goal was to hire and train local staff as rapidly as possible. Then, as now, the cost of maintaining expatriate staff was a burden.

The late Howard G. (Scotty) Sawyer, a long-time Marsteller advertising executive, was temporarily assigned to open Brussels – both public relations and advertising. Scotty had never traveled outside the U.S. but he quickly learned how to do business in Europe. Weighing barely a hundred pounds, he was effective at selling new business and usually crafted his winning proposals in the wee hours following late afternoon calls on prospective clients. His successor was an earnest 29-year-old New Yorker, Robert S. (Bob) Leaf, hired by Buck Buchwald as our first trainee in 1958. For the next quarter century, Leaf led our overseas growth. When he stepped down as international CEO in the early 1990s, Burson-Marsteller was the premier public relations firm in both Europe and Asia.

For almost two decades B-M's Brussels office was a training ground for general managers of our newly-established overseas offices. Eric Sjogren, who joined us from the Swedish airline SAS, was dispatched to Frankfurt to head up our German operations. In short order, Chris Fisher, a Brit, went to Paris where he remained (save three years when he was our resident executive at EXPO92 in Seville) until he retired after the start of the new century. The late Michael Horton was general manager in both Canada (based in Toronto) and London. Mike Sperring went from Brussels to Tokyo and then to Sydney. All had worked together as group executives under Bob Leaf's tutelage during the decades of the 1960s and 1970s.

Our Brussels business grew rapidly as U.S. corporations moved to Europe in droves – to Germany, to England, to Holland, to France, to Italy, to Spain. Returned from Europe, Scotty Sawyer scanned the business pages for news of U.S. firms going abroad and followed up with new business calls. We often made the sale before clients reached their new overseas offices, and designing and ordering new stationery was frequently our first assignment.

In 1994, with the growing regulatory function of the European Commission affecting all manner of business transactions, we equipped ourselves to provide a comprehensive public affairs service to clients by acquiring Robinson-Linton, a highly regarded firm in the political sector. Since that time, Robinson Linton, now operating as BKSH (a wholly owned B-M subsidiary headquartered in Washington) has served clients on significant regulatory and political issues.

For about 15 years, client needs in Holland were handled by Dutch-speaking professionals in our Brussels office (Amsterdam and Rotterdam are short train rides). But in 1981, Ferry de Bakker, a talented and dynamic Hollander who had joined us in Singapore five years earlier, returned to the country of his birth and opened an office in The Hague. With a staff of about 30 at the end of the decade, it was regarded as one of our most creative offices and served a variety of multinational clients like Unilever and other large Dutch enterprises like Akzo. Ferry went on to be European CEO and then Asia/Pacific CEO before retiring at the end of the century.

⤜⫘⤛

We established our third European outpost in London. While I had played a significant role in putting our London affiliate, Roles & Parker, in the public relations business, the working relationship between our organizations was a textbook case of "two peoples separated by a common language." Roles & Parker professionals considered American strategy and tactics too aggressive and out of context for a British audience; while my American colleagues thought the Brits were forever committed to the "not invented here" syndrome and prone to inaction and the status quo.

Peter Parker, the Roles & Parker chairman, was not of a mind to throw in the towel. He had joined our board of directors, a quid pro quo for my being on his board, and relished his quarterly visits to the United States (I enjoyed my London visits with him because he put his chauffeured Jaguar at my disposal!). The two of us had a friendly relationship throughout our five-year association and often discussed the deep-seated differences and disputes at the working level of our two organizations. One simple example was his unyielding notion that a British client would never "accept" an American account executive, no matter how competent. He insisted that all contact with our shared British clients, even subsidiaries of U.S. companies, be undertaken by members of his U.K. staff. Without telling him, I queried a couple of clients in London and found the opposite to be true – similar to clients everywhere, they wanted new ideas and new approaches without regard to national origin.

I came to the conclusion we must have our own office in London despite Pete Parker's refusal to acknowledge that the cultures and work styles of our two businesses were irreconcilable. Knowing he would react strongly to my unilateral decision to terminate the relationship, I met with him over dinner at the Ritz Hotel in London one quiet Sunday evening in July 1967. He was surprised when I told him my decision was non-negotiable, and he very reluctantly accepted the one-year separation notice provided for in our contract. He was palpably disappointed because he had hoped we would eventually purchase his company. Instead, he repurchased the fifteen percent interest we held and we again made a profit on the transaction.

The actual timing to pull out of the Roles & Parker relationship was triggered by a telephone call from John Addey, the colorful co-owner of C.S. Services, a mid-sized London public relations firm. Addey had visited me in New York five years earlier and we had seen one another many times since. Addey's partner was Claude Simmonds, once Parliamentary Secretary to the former Chancellor of the Exchequer Sir Stafford Cripps. A prototypical English country gentleman nearing his 65th birthday, Simmonds wanted to retire. This necessitated selling his half interest in the firm. Addey had the right of first refusal, but he lacked ready cash to buy out his partner. Also, Addey had told me many times that his ultimate goal was to be part of a larger international public relations business, hopefully Burson-Marsteller.

Leaf and I quickly reached agreement for C.S. Services. We paid about

$100,000 for Simmond's half interest and swapped Addey's C.S. Services shares for our shares on a basis somewhat favorable to him. After a short interval, we dropped the C.S. Services name and began to do business as Burson-Marsteller in an office located in London's West End across the street from the fashionable Connaught Hotel. Despite the classy neighborhood, 5 Carlos Place provided a less than ideal layout for a thirty-person public relations firm. It was a five-story Victorian town house, once a single-family home, with no elevator and minimal usable floor space. Most of the business seemed to be conducted on the spiral staircase. Barely a year later, in 1968, we moved to another impressive address at 73-75 Jermyn Street, occupying 9,000 square feet on two floors of a six-story building owned by the Church of England. Bob Leaf, who negotiated the lease, later spoke of "the nice people who gave us a break on the rent." In fact, when we moved into larger space on North Row, near the Selfridge department store, three years later, we realized a substantial profit selling the lease.

Through John Addey's efforts, we were involved in a high profile hostile takeover shortly after our arrival in London. Our client was Rupert Murdoch, who was making his first move to establish himself as a major Fleet Street publisher with a hostile tender offer for the *News of the World* tabloid. Bidding against him in a bitter widely fought contest for majority control was Robert Maxwell, who was then building his own publishing empire. In *The Wall Street Journal* article reporting on Murdoch's victory, John Addey, identified as managing director of Burson-Marsteller's London office, was said to have organized an "anti-Maxwell claque" that was "rude" to Maxwell during his presentation to stockholders. Fearing my wrath because one of our senior managers had been rude in a public setting, Bob telephoned to assure me that Addey's tactics, though a bit extreme, were a significant factor in Murdoch's successful takeover. Through the years, Bob has expressed surprise at my reply. As Bob puts it, "in his deepest Southern drawl, Harold said 'Bob, now everyone knows that we have a London office that is doing significant work and I already have gotten some telephone calls about it.'" We became a major presence on the London public relations scene early on.

Entering a country by acquiring an existing agency was aberrational behavior for me. My goal was to build a company with a single culture worldwide – a goal most effectively reached by growing organically. My rationale for taking the acquisition route in London was that I considered it important to enter the mature London public relations scene with "mass" – an established client roster and an ongoing business. Also, I was attracted to C.S. Services because I knew John Addey and because the firm's clients were in the consumer product/services sector, among them Beefeater Gin, Vidal Sassoon (cosmetics), Burberry and Austin Reed (department stores). This was in keeping with our plan to broaden our range of services beyond business-to business. To instill what was even at that early date an incipient identifiable Burson-Marsteller culture, Bob Leaf made weekly visits to our newest office before taking permanent residence in London a year after the acquisition. He quickly discovered that most of the staff failed to meet our standards and within eighteen months only five remained. Among those hired as replacements were Reginald Watts, who later headed the office for more than a decade, and Martin Langford, whose thirty-year career included stays at B-M/Hong Kong and B-M/Singapore. Claude Simmonds, after selling his shares to us, postponed his retirement and spent a productive five years with us.

Of the many "Bob Leaf stories," one I like happened during one of his frequent trips from Brussels to London. On arriving at Heathrow, the immigration officer, with deliberation and visible suspicion, warily eyed Bob and then his passport, looking at Bob's passport and then at Bob and then repeating the process. Realizing something was amiss, six-footer Bob leaned across the counter and quickly saw he had mistakenly presented his five-year-old son's passport. Pointing his finger, Bob explained, "That's an old photo," looking the flabbergasted immigration officer straight in the eye. He was allowed to enter the U.K.

During the decade of the 1970s, B-M/Brussels was the "crown jewel" of our overseas business, the largest Burson-Marsteller office outside the United States. It was a truly international operation that turned out work in a dozen languages. In delivering a pan-European service it routinely prepared and placed articles in publications across Europe, including the Soviet Union. In so doing, the office was simply adapting to the needs of multinational clients whose distributors and customers did business in a multitude of languages.

The operating model of American companies of that era was to establish a regional headquarters, frequently in Brussels, headed by Americans and staffed by local nationals. The intent, especially for business-to-business companies, was to manage their Europe-wide business from a single location. Marketing executives worked with distributors or agents in the various European countries and controlled advertising, promotion and public relations from headquarters. This worked well until increased sales signaled a market's importance to either the

manufacturer or the local distributor. Invariably, sales management in larger mar
kets like Germany, France, the United Kingdom and Italy sought greater freedom
from regional headquarters – not to speak of their own budgets and control ove
advertising and public relations. We had anticipated this evolution in our clients
marketing strategies and began preparing ourselves to fulfill their public relation
needs country-by-country.

∞∞∞

Our first office in Germany came into being in 1972 in Stuttgart afte
Marsteller Advertising bought the Bruder agency. We thought it only natural to
offer public relations services to Bruder clients and several hired us. The next year
we moved two Stuttgart staffers to Frankfurt as the nucleus of a new office head
ed by Eric Sjogren, transferred from Brussels. He was manager of our Frankfur
office for the remainder of the decade. After winning a major assignment in 197?
to promote Berlin's 700th anniversary, we opened a small office in the one-tim·
German capital but it was closed two years later when the project was complet
ed. We reopened the Berlin office in 1990 after the removal of the Berlin Wal
and the restoration of Berlin as Germany's capital city. The office now provide
public affairs services under the BKSH banner.

Germany, the largest economy in Europe, has always been a difficult marke
for public relations firms. Prior to our entry – my recollection is that Burson
Marsteller was the first international firm to establish an office in Germany – th·
typical large German company had a well-populated, self-sufficient public rela
tions department. Some, like Siemens and Bayer and automobile companies lik·
Mercedes-Benz, Volkswagen and BMW, had departments of up to a hundred
people. A few highly regarded public relations counselors advised these larg·
companies as well as other institutions. These consultants were often students o·
the opinion-formation process deeply immersed in opinion formation and com
munications theory.

Our operations in Germany grew slowly although we got considerable recog
nition for our pioneering role. Our clients were predominantly U.S. and U.K
multinationals like Unilever (introducing their low cholesterol margarine) and
Dow Chemical, which had a large manufacturing facility in Germany. We added
a Hamburg office in 1982 and it developed a strong healthcare capability to serv·
such clients as Johnson & Johnson's Ethicon Division. Another small office wa
opened in Bonn to provide public affairs services. After recruiting Jurgen

Togotzes from Schering A.G., the large German pharmaceutical company, in the early 1980s, our business expanded considerably. For a short time at the end of the decade, we were the largest public relations firm in Germany after acquiring Conti Public Relations, based in Munich. This acquisition proved to be an expensive mistake. We operated the thirty-person business for two years before closing the office and taking a substantial write-off. Conti had a small office in Vienna, also closed after two years.

∞≫∞

In 1976 Chris Fisher, one of the pioneer B-M/Brussels group managers, opened a Paris office and remained there until his retirement a quarter century later. I had lived in Paris for five months immediately following the end of the war in Europe as a member of the news staff of American Forces Network. Our headquarters was at 19 Avenue de Iena, residence of the German ambassador during the occupation. The timing of my stay in Paris was perhaps the best ever for an unwed young American!

Like Germany, France was also a difficult and unexplored market for international public relations firms. Unlike Germany, which had not at that time nurtured a single sizeable firm, France boasted a strong public relations consultancy headed by a charismatic former press chief to General Charles de Gaulle during and immediately following World War II. His firm, still in existence, had a staff of about thirty when we entered the market and continues to be the largest public relations firm in France.

For more than a decade B-M/Paris mainly served multinational clients with French operations. Two acquisitions gave Burson-Marsteller the credentials to compete as a French agency and gain some important French companies as clients, among them Rhône-Poulenc and L'Oreal. The first, in which we acquired a forty-nine percent interest in 1988, was Londez Conseil, a specialist in financial public relations. Although we subsequently acquired the remainder of the shares in Londez Conseil, the cultures of our two firms never meshed and we sold the business in the mid-1990s. Financially, we came out even. A more successful acquisition in 1995 was Eurocorporate, a specialist in corporate relations headed by Jean-Pierre Rousset. This move reinvigorated our French operations and made us one of the country's larger and most respected firms. For most of its existence, B-M/Paris was quartered in the Champs Elysee area. In 2000, the office moved to Boulogne Billancourt on the outskirts of Paris, a move necessitated by steeply escalating midtown rents.

Burson-Marsteller began an affiliation in Spain in the 1970s with a small firm owned by the late Bernard Jennings, a transplanted American who once operat ed a public relations business in pre-Castro Havana. As Spain's economic impor tance grew after it joined the European Community, the Jennings firm was too small to service the growing needs of B-M clients. The situation was exacerbated when Jennings became terminally ill with cancer.

For several years, B-M managers in Europe had worked successfully with a Jennings junior staffer, Teresa Dorn, an American with a passionate interest in Spain. Her first visit was as a University of Wisconsin exchange student and she literally never returned to the U.S. to live. Realizing she had outgrown Jennings from a career standpoint, she resigned in 1981, and Bob Leaf quickly asked her to start a Burson-Marsteller office in Madrid. Less than a decade later, after adding an office in Barcelona, Burson-Marsteller became Spain's largest public relations firm with a totally Spanish staff and a strong Spanish client base. Over the past two decades, we have been the market leader in that country, our visibil ity heightened when we were selected to manage the public relations function for EXPO92 in Seville. The versatile Chris Fisher was EXPO's resident chief public relations officer for three years and Burson-Marsteller also represented several major exhibitors. Our Madrid business has continued to flourish under the lead ership of Carlos Lareau, who now heads B-M operations on the Continent.

In the late 1990s, we established a small office in Lisbon, a successful mini office until the economic downturn in 2002 when the office was closed and its activities transferred to Madrid.

In 1982, Burson-Marsteller opened its own office in Italy in a manner some what akin to how we got started in Spain. For years, we relied on a succession of small Italian public relations firms to cover the Italian market. For the most part we were less than satisfied with our affiliates, an evaluation that fit many of the loose affiliations Burson-Marsteller has had with other public relations firms both in the United States and around the world. This negative experience seldom reflects a lack of competence or professionalism on the part of the affiliate Rather, these relationships usually lack the financial substance and incentive to make them important to both parties. In setting us up in Italy, Leaf acted on rumors of management discord at our competitor, Hill & Knowlton, whose

Milan office was then tops in Italy. Gigliola Ibba, a motivated Milan native schooled both in strategic public relations and in managing a public relations business, was the person behind that success. Leaf hired her to start a B-M office in Italy. Within a decade, and after opening a public affairs office in Rome, Burson-Marsteller was the country's market leader.

The aftermath of the two oil crises in 1973 and 1978 spurred several of our larger clients, including American Express and Citicorp, to establish themselves in the newly (but briefly) thriving Middle East. While we had not identified that part of the world as a market for our services, several of the region's leading advertising agencies encouraged us to form alliances with them to establish Burson-Marsteller offices in the Arab world. The most persistent was Intermarkets, whose senior executives made repeated visits to New York and London to press their case with me and Bob Leaf. With headquarters in Beirut, Intermarkets had the Middle East's largest advertising network. We joined forces with them in 1979 and treated the venture as an extension of our European operation.

Our strategy called for setting up a small regional Burson-Marsteller/Intermarkets office in Bahrain staffed by professionals from our two companies. This office would serve as a central planning and coordinating resource and draw on Intermarket offices in Lebanon, Syria, Egypt, Saudi Arabia and the Gulf Emirates to implement client assignments. We also made plans to open a Burson-Marsteller office in Beirut. In fact, the civil war in Lebanon broke out the day after Bob Leaf finalized arrangements and, of course, the idea was abandoned.

The Bahrain office was in business for three years before client interest in the Gulf area waned. We closed our office in 1983 and reverted to depending on our affiliate, Intermarkets, to fulfill client needs. Bill Rylance, now CEO of B-M's Asia-Pacific Region, spent two years at B-M/Bahrain before moving to Korea to lead our work for the Seoul Olympic Organizing Committee for the 1988 Summer Games and, subsequently, to his present post in Hong Kong as CEO of Asia-Pacific. We "tested" the market with our own small office in 1996 when Allan Biggar, now CEO of B-M/London, was sent to Cairo. The impetus was a contract from the Egyptian Tourist agency to rekindle European travel in Egypt. Although the office played a substantive client-service role, we quickly concluded that the market was not yet ripe for a fully-staffed office.

Scandinavia tempted us for many years – both for the potential in Europe and for Swedish multinationals operating around the world. Bob Leaf and I made numerous exploratory visits, primarily to Stockholm, before deciding to enter into an arrangement in 1981 with a small public relations firm in Malmo to represent us in Stockholm. It worked for a year or so, but it became obvious that we would have to make a relatively significant investment in staff. Unexpectedly Young & Rubicam provided the key that soon made us a major player in Scandinavia. Y&R owned Norway's largest public relations firm, Planned Public Relations (PPR), the result of an advertising agency acquisition ten years earlier. PPR changed its name and our European staff took on 40 new people and more than $4 million in income. As part of its public relations business, PPR was Norway's premier designer of exhibits and trade shows. Trond Andresen was general manager of the Oslo business and he quickly accepted the challenge of establishing a Burson-Marsteller presence in Stockholm. B-M/Oslo has been one of our most creative offices and played a major role in helping Lillehammer win the venue competition for the 1994 Olympic Winter Games.

A Copenhagen office was added in 1985 and was strengthened with the acquisition of Brinkmann Kommunications in 1988. Major Brinkmann clients included the Danish Post Office and Tuborg beer. Burson-Marsteller became the largest public relations firm in Scandinavia with income in excess of $10 million.

Our most recent expansion in Europe was in the countries once dominated by the Soviet Union. Actually, we were in Moscow before the dissolution of the U.S.S.R. in two unconnected situations. The first was during the Cold War "détente" interval when President Richard Nixon and Secretary of State Henry Kissinger sought to reduce tensions with the Soviet Union. Our presence resulted from speeches on public relations Bob Leaf delivered in the early 1970s in Bucharest, Prague, Warsaw and Moscow. In the audience were representatives of Vneshtorgreklama, the Soviet state advertising agency. They hired Burson-Marsteller to represent their trade magazines in the U.S., an assignment that continued for three years and B-M/Los Angeles helped facilitate the big exposition in 1977 that marked the U.S.S.R.'s 60th anniversary.

Subsequently, in 1989, Mike Adams moved from B-M/Chicago to Moscow to become Russia's first western public relations professional. Officially, Mike headed a joint venture between Young & Rubicam and Vnestorgreklama, our former client. Soon after the dissolution of the Soviet Union, we established B-M offices in Moscow, Almaty in Khazakstan and Kiev in Ukraine. They worked largely on privatization projects and other public sector initiatives financed by the World Bank and the U.S. Agency for Industrial Development. At peak in the late 1990s, we had about one hundred and sixty employees in the countries of the former Soviet Union. Soon after the fall of the Berlin Wall, we opened offices in Budapest, Warsaw and Prague and became the premier public relations firm in that part of Europe.

After the start of the new century, B-M management decided the potential in central and Eastern Europe did not justify wholly-owned Burson-Marsteller offices. Employee managers of five offices were provided an opportunity to acquire ownership of these offices and continue to work alongside Burson-Marsteller as affiliates. Mike Willard took over the Kiev (Ukraine) and Moscow offices; Michal Donath took Prague; Y&R Poland, including several former Burson-Marsteller employees, took Warsaw; and a group of B-M employees continued to operate the Budapest office.

———— ∞∞∞ ————

With the retirement of Claude Marshall in 1993 and a sharp reduction in revenues due to the transfer of several international accounts to B-M/London, our Geneva office was closed thirty-two years after it became our first overseas location. In the 1980s, we established a corporate/financial outpost in Zurich with a staff of six people. Its operations were at a low level and the office was closed in favor of an affiliation with Jäggi Communications, a leading Swiss public relations/public affairs firm which also had an office in Berne. In 1997, we acquired the Jäggi business and it has operated as Burson-Marsteller in Switzerland since then.

———— ∞∞∞ ————

Our "most significant defining moment" – that's the importance I attach to opening a Burson-Marsteller office in Geneva in 1961.

At that time, our annual revenues were less than a million dollars. Although there were no published rankings, it would be a stretch to say we were among the top twenty-five public relations firms. Hill & Knowlton was the largest and the only firm with offices in Europe. By establishing ourselves in Geneva, Burson-Marsteller became the "other" international public relations firm. For us, it was a powerful differentiator that had a positive impact on our growth and reputation.

We now have sixteen offices in eleven countries in Europe. They account for twenty-five to thirty percent of our global revenue. B-M/London is our third largest office. Until 1990, Burson-Marsteller and Hill & Knowlton were the dominant pan-Europe firms. Since that time, the other top ten firms have entered the market, mostly by acquiring local firms.

Also noteworthy was the success of Marsteller Advertising. Like Burson-Marsteller, it started in Geneva then expanded to Brussels, London, Paris and Frankfurt. Bob March, who briefly headed both advertising and public relations in Geneva, was succeeded by Reginald Bird, who managed the advertising business until the mid-1980s when the business was consolidated into Y&R. Bob Trebus and Lou Magnani, who both came from Marsteller Advertising's New York office, made B-M/Brussels one of the major agencies in Belgium. The late Peter Johns was hired in London and built an organization of a hundred people with clients like Mercedes on his roster. Like Geneva, the other Marsteller offices in Europe were taken over by Y&R.

The aspect of our achievement that amazes me is that a couple dozen (at most) pioneering B-Mers created a seamless network of offices with so small a financial investment. Businesses in Switzerland, Belgium, Germany, France, Spain, Italy and the Netherlands were all created by giving B-M professionals assignments to start offices and, in effect, to "live off the land" while doing so. In the other countries, mainly the U.K., our investments were minimal. In just about every country, we are among the market leaders serving both multinational and local clients. And in Europe as elsewhere, there's no better credential than having Burson-Marsteller on one's resume when seeking a position in public relations!

Chapter 6

◆◆◆

The Next Steps in Going Global: Offices in Asia and Australia

A s we entered the decade of the 1970s, our business was booming in the U.S. and growing in Europe, mainly from client referrals and unsolicited calls from companies seeking our services. We had grown 48 percent in 1966, 42 percent in 1967, 25 percent in 1968 and 26 percent in 1969. Our revenues in 1970 exceeded $5 million and, in 1971, the first year Jack O'Dwyer listed public relations firms by fee income, our $6,006,000 ranked us as the third largest firm behind Hill & Knowlton and Ruder·Finn. The following year, we ranked second after our twelfth consecutive year of double-digit growth.

In the U.S., we boasted a nationwide presence. The three offices we opened in the 1950s – New York, Chicago and Pittsburgh – had been augmented with operations in Los Angeles and Washington. We were in Toronto and had a firm foothold in Europe with offices in Geneva, Brussels and London. Only one other firm, Hill & Knowlton, had broader geographic reach. We were not only "the other international public relations firm" but also the fastest growing.

Our goal to become a truly global business had not changed. That meant starting a business in Asia, a part of the world that was then almost as remote to me as the moon. My initial cognizance of Asia, as with many U.S. executives, was largely a result of observing Japanese auto, stereo-TV and camera manufacturers capture significant shares of the U.S. market. I was somewhat aware of the economic growth in Southeast Asia because our New York office was working (with a high degree of success) with the Singapore Economic Development Board promoting U.S. investment in that newly-formed island nation. Asia, other than potential Japanese competition, was just becoming a top-of-mind subject among client executives.

Starting in 1970, I began talking about our Asia plans with Bob Leaf, by then based in London and productively occupied expanding our operations on the Continent. Neither of us had a clear-cut idea on how to proceed in Asia, nor had either of us been there for a firsthand appraisal. Intuitively, I thought we should start with an office in Tokyo because Japan was far-and-away the largest market at a time when an "open" China was not yet on anyone's radar screen. In fact, several owners of Japanese public relations firms had sought me out during visits to New York to discuss affiliations with them. Usually, they wanted to represent Burson-Marsteller in Japan (which actually meant referring business from our clients). That was far from my objective – which was to establish a strong B-M presence in Tokyo, preferably a joint venture with a Japanese partner. Committed to providing a global service for multinational clients, I felt it was essential for us to manage any operation we set up in Asia. Actually, our entry into Asia came about suddenly and unexpectedly in a way that was far afield from our early thinking.

Seeking to expand our contacts around the world, Bob Leaf and I signed up for the International Public Relations Association (IPRA) world conference in May 1972. After an opening session in Oslo, we boarded a boat for what was to become a befogged two-day sail through the Norwegian fjords. Shortly after leaving dockside, Leaf appeared in the bar with a goateed gentleman, the spitting image of King George V. He was Peter Bostock, and like King George, an Englishman. Honeymooning with his new bride (his fourth), a lovely Chinese lady whose name is Kiat, Peter managed the Singapore public relations unit of a now-defunct but once thriving business in Asia, Grant Advertising. We were soon joined by his boss, David Mitchell, an Australian based in Hong Kong who headed Grant's Asian public relations unit. In his first ten minutes with them, Leaf learned they had decided to leave Grant because of a change in ownership that was unsympathetic to the public relations part of the business. In fact, Mitchell and Bostock signed up for the IPRA conference because they knew that Leaf and I would be there.

David Mitchell and Peter Bostock are among the most colorful (as well as competent) professionals ever associated with Burson-Marsteller. Their proposition was simple: they wanted to launch Burson-Marsteller in Asia. They were confident they could muster both staff and clients for an immediately profitable start-up. Patiently, they explained that establishing offices in Hong Kong and Singapore had priority over an office in Tokyo and was sure to be more profitable. All they required was the Burson-Marsteller name, a modest amount of working capital, office space and a telephone system. Give them the word and we would soon be in business in Hong Kong and Singapore and on our way to a preeminent position in Asia. They also put forth the possibility that we might be able to convince their Grant counterpart in Tokyo to jump ship and join the new Burson-Marsteller Asian upstart. If successful, we would be starting our business in Asia with three offices – an auspicious beginning with minimal cash investment.

As the IPRA voyage/conference ended, Leaf and I accepted the Mitchell/Bostock proposal and aimed for an early 1973 start-up in Hong Kong and Singapore. We agreed to a joint venture owned 60 percent by Burson-Marsteller and 20 percent each by Mitchell and Bostock. We invited them to visit New York in August to finalize the agreement and meet Bill Marsteller and other B-M executives and agreed to pay for their trip (economy tickets). They arrived in New York and promptly charmed all concerned. The few remaining business details were dispatched with ease. They then spent a week learning Burson-Marsteller policies and procedures and absorbing the culture. Their insights on how the public relations business in Asia was likely to evolve proved to be remarkably on target, and they correctly predicted that Burson-Marsteller would become the region's premier public relations firm within five-to-ten years. The only serious Pan-Asia (and Australian) competition at the time was Hill & Knowlton, which had acquired Eric White & Partners, an Australian-headquartered firm then the world's third largest public relations business. Mitchell and Bostock considered H&K vulnerable in Asia due to the departure of several key people.

We agreed that Burson-Marsteller offices would open for business in Hong Kong and Singapore on February 1, 1973. Leaf and I attended the opening festivities. For me, it was the first of about forty visits to Asia and, for

Leaf, the forerunner of even more trips and, toward the end of his career with Burson-Marsteller, a three-year assignment in Hong Kong. As the opening date approached, the new owner of Grant Advertising's Asian business, a Toronto-based company, indicated through legal channels his displeasure at the loss not only of Mitchell and Bostock but also the eventuality of losing more of their people and some clients. From the time we started talking with them, I anticipated that their proposition might subject us to a lawsuit. Accordingly, I insisted that they obtain legal counsel in Hong Kong and Singapore and I consulted our own lawyer every step along the way. On both sides of the Pacific, attorneys assured us we would prevail in a lawsuit if we followed the procedures we had all agreed on. However, we were happy to dispose of the matter by paying Grant $50,000 in return for an agreement to forego any legal action against us. It was the biggest bargain ever for Burson-Marsteller.

The first stop of the Burson/Leaf Asian visit in late January was Tokyo where Mitchell had arranged for us to meet their Grant associate, the late Bill Fish. Mitchell hoped the Burson/Leaf combination would remove Fish's doubts about joining the new venture. Fish, however, was determined to stay the course with Grant. Accordingly, Tokyo temporarily remained an unfilled "dot on the map" for Burson-Marsteller. Leaf and I proceeded to Hong Kong and Singapore where we spent ten days meeting staff, the several clients who promised to follow Mitchell and Bostock, numerous prospects, including B-M U.S. and European clients, and the media. Our first Hong Kong client was Bank of America (B of A), an important win for us because B of A was the leading U.S. financial services business in Asia at the time.

Newspapers in Hong Kong and Singapore treated our entry into the Asian market with headlines as large as those that heralded Coca-Cola and McDonald's arrival in China. For several days running, interviews and articles reflected the close connections our two new colleagues had with Asian media. They tried to outdo one another with lavish menus for client, staff and prospect dinners and receptions, including ten-course formal Chinese banquets at the Mandarin Hotel in Hong Kong and the Shangri-La in Singapore. Our Asian business was off to a good start with a staff of fourteen in Hong Kong and ten in Singapore. Almost all of them had worked with Mitchell or Bostock at Grant. Both offices showed a profit the first year, a situation somewhat different from our experience in Europe. Both men were capable financial managers and their 20 percent individual ownership gave them a strong incentive to operate profitably.

Before we left Singapore, Peter Bostock informed us that we would soon require an office in Kuala Lumpur. In the most far-fetched business scenario I could ever have conjured up, I would never have thought that Burson-Marsteller would one day have an office in Malaysia. With considerable patience, Bostock explained the close ties between Singapore and its neighbor Malaysia. Because of our work for the Singapore Economic Development Board (as well as from reading *The New York Times*), I knew that Singapore had seceded from Malaysia in the early 1960s. But I failed to appreciate that the economies of the two nations were so closely tied to one another. In July, we opened a small office in the Malaysian capital, Kuala Lumpur. It was temporarily headed by Robert (Bob) Bussjaeger, a retired Vietnam War veteran who had been General Westmoreland's public information officer. During the several months we searched for space, our office was in a hotel suite that also housed a cot where Bussjaeger slept. Two early hires were CT Hew, who eventually headed our Asia/Australia operations after two years in London, and Jacqui Chan, who later married Peter Walford when he was manager of B-M/ Tokyo. Godfrey Scotchbrook, today regarded as one of Asia's most experienced public relations counselors, took over from Bob Bussjaeger and four years later became head of B-M operations in Hong Kong and then all of Asia.

Although I tried to resist considering myself an expert on Asia after a single visit, I believed that a viable operation in Japan required a respected Japanese partner. After meeting several Japanese public relations firms, the small firms seemed inadequate for our needs and the larger firms showed little interest in having Burson-Marsteller as a partner in their home market. In the course of my talks, which included a second visit to Japan, I learned that Fuji Bank, then Japan's second largest bank, owned an advertising agency subsidiary headed by Keizo Iwasa, son of the well-known and highly respected Fuji Bank chairman. After meeting Keizo, I proposed establishing a jointly-owned public relations business which Burson-Marsteller would manage. In effect, we would be starting our own office with well-established Japanese sponsorship. Several weeks later, the chairman of Fuji Bank sent me a Telex message inviting me to join him for tea at the Hotel Pierre in New York. It was hard to believe the chairman of one of the world's largest banks would engage me in negotiations to establish a small jointly-owned public relations firm in Tokyo, but that's what happened.

After some small talk about politics and the economy, Chairman Yoshizani Iwasa asked through his interpreter how much capital would be needed to start a public relations business in Japan. I told him $100,000 should be adequate, not knowing that a tenant renting office space in Tokyo must ante up a year's rent in escrow. Mr. Iwasa agreed that $100,000 seemed reasonable for initial capitalization and said Fuji Bank would loan the new company funds to cover the rental security deposit and the cost of new furniture and equipment. We then discussed equity ownership. I proposed an eighty/twenty division; he countered with seventy/thirty. I accepted and we had a deal.

The meeting, in retrospect, had a great deal of fantasy about it – something akin to negotiating with David Rockefeller to establish a five-person business on the other side of the world. But it started a personal relationship between me and the Iwasa family that has continued through the years. (The senior Mr. Iwasa died in 2002 at the age of 95.) When in Tokyo, my wife and I were regularly invited to the Iwasa home for dinner. Though forewarned by Japan "experts" that it would take "several years to become profitable," the company we named Burson-Marsteller/Fuji was in the black its first year.

Anticipating a Tokyo office, we hired two young professionals – one in New York, the other in London – and put them through a training program that would enable them to transfer B-M methodology and culture to Japan. One was Satoshi Sugita, a business news reporter on *The Cincinnati Post*, who, after reading that we planned a Tokyo office, telephoned me to talk about joining Burson-Marsteller. Born and educated in Tokyo, with a master's degree in journalism from Ohio State University, Satoshi's objective after four years in the U.S. was to return to Tokyo with a U.S. employer. We bought him a ticket to New York for an interview and hired him immediately. He worked at B-M/New York for six months before relocating to our new office in Japan. Concurrently, Paul Adams, an Australian who received the Japanese equivalent of a Rhodes scholarship and studied in Tokyo, had joined B-M/London. His facility in spoken and written Japanese made him a natural choice for our new Tokyo office. Both arrived for the opening of our office in November 1973.

The account-handling team was augmented by Makoto Yagi, who came to us from United Press International and remained with B-M/Tokyo for the next twenty-five years. Another long timer, some twenty years, was Gerry Simmel, who transferred from B-M/Hong Kong. Our first general manager in Tokyo was Peter Walford, whose thirty-year career with Burson-Marsteller started at B-M/Geneva. Peter was Burson-Marsteller's most gifted linguist. He spoke ten languages, including Mandarin and Russian, and I felt he would quickly learn Japanese. He headed the office for seven years before moving to Sydney. Learning Japanese, he said, was the toughest language challenge he ever faced.

The lavish reception celebrating our opening was attended by the heads of major Japanese companies as well as U.S. and European multinationals. It received extensive press coverage that included photos of Chairman Iwasa and me. Our new business effort got a boost when client and prospective CEOs were invited for lunch in the private dining room of the chairman of the Fuji Bank when they visited Tokyo. Unilever, an early client, hired us to promote Rama margarine. We successfully used the same public relations strategy that had proven so successful for Unilever's Flora margarine in the United Kingdom.

Within five years, Mr. Iwasa Sr. retired as Fuji Bank chairman and his son, Keizo, left the bank's advertising subsidiary to pursue other interests. While relations with our joint venture partner remained cordial, Fuji Bank's participation in our joint venture was severely diminished. Absent the chairman's personal interest, owning a minority interest in a single office of an American public relations firm was an aberration for Fuji Bank and provided no benefit to us. In the early 1980s, we offered to repurchase their thirty percent holding. As a face-saving device for the Fuji ad subsidiary's new manager, we agreed that the Fuji stock interest would first be reduced from thirty percent to twenty percent and that the subject would be revisited within two years. For ten percent of the stock, Fuji Bank received $69,000. Their total original investment was $30,000. Two years later, we regained one hundred percent ownership upon payment of an additional $200,000, a reflection of growth in book value. It had been a good financial deal for both us and the Fuji Bank.

In 1989, after Jim Dowling succeeded me as CEO, we entered into a relationship with Dentsu, Japan's largest and most prestigious advertising agency, whereby our two companies shared ownership of B-M/Tokyo and a new U.S. agency called Dentsu/Burson-Marsteller. In addition to the fact that our parent company Young & Rubicam and Dentsu were partners in Asia and shared ownership of an advertising agency in the United States called DYR (which included Marsteller Advertising), Burson-Marsteller had two reasons for joining forces with Dentsu. First, though B-M/Tokyo had been profitable from the outset, fee income had leveled off for the past four or five years. While we won our share of business from U.S. and European companies, we had never been able to develop a significant relationship with a major Japanese company. My associates felt that an affiliation with Dentsu would help us win Japanese clients. Second,

Dentsu/Burson-Marsteller, set up offices in Los Angeles and New York to serve Japanese clients marketing their products in the United States. D/B-M also offered a public affairs service. The joint venture lasted until 1997 when we repurchased our shares in B-M/Tokyo and disbanded Dentsu/Burson-Marsteller after failing to reach either objective. Our Tokyo office still lacked a major Japanese company as a client and Japanese companies did not embrace the idea of working with a jointly-owned Japan/U.S. public relations/public affairs firm in the U.S. Burson-Marsteller resumed full ownership of B-M/Tokyo and, a couple years later, installed our first Japanese general manager, Tsuyoshi (TT) Takemura.

A change in ownership and management of the Southeast Asia offices occurred in the late 1970s. David Mitchell, who headed both the Asian region and the Hong Kong office, was offered the job of chief public relations officer for the World Wildlife Fund (WWF) in Switzerland. For Mitchell, it was tempting both professionally and for family reasons. His children were of school age and he preferred that they be educated in Europe. Also, his German-born wife, Renata, would be closer to her family. The WWF position entailed working closely with Prince Philip, WWF international chairman, and a host of world-class business leaders to achieve the organization's environmental goals of saving endangered species and preserving endangered habitats. Mitchell took the job and sold his twenty percent minority interest to the company. Peter Bostock became Asia Regional CEO and remained in Singapore. For five years I was on the WWF board amidst royalty and multi-millionaire industrialists.

Having become a major player in Hong Kong with a staff of seventy-five people during our first decade in Asia, we began to eye mainland China as a potentially important market for our services. At the time, 1985, foreign-owned firms establishing themselves in China were required to associate themselves with a Chinese joint venture partner. Our Hong Kong general manager, Godfrey Scotchbrook, and his second-in-command, Sam Lam, came up with the novel idea of joint venturing with the official Chinese news agency, Xinhua. For several years, Xinhua had operated photography and printing and translation services that catered to Western business customers. Together, we established China Global Public Relations, a new public relations firm owned by Xinhua but managed at the outset by B-M/Hong Kong. Xinhua provided tactical staff which worked under our supervision to implement projects for B-M clients in China. This arrangement had obvious advantages, among them Xinhua's ministerial status as China's official news agency which gave our clients access to both media and government officials. The agreement also required Burson-Marsteller to train China Global staffers. This was done mainly in Hong Kong for two to four trainees per year. Several came to New York for stays of a few months.

The Xinhua contract specified an eight-year relationship. China Global Public Relations would then operate independently and Burson-Marsteller would be free to open its own office in China. China Global's long-term objective was to prepare itself to represent local Chinese businesses while Burson-Marsteller's aim was to serve multinational clients doing business in China. Both parties were satisfied with the collaboration. When the agreement terminated in 1993, Burson-Marsteller opened its own offices in Beijing, Shanghai and Guangzhou although we had effectively operated in China since 1985. Scott Seligman, who joined B-M/Washington after several years with the U.S.-China Business Council in Beijing and Taipei, transferred to B-M/Beijing and played a significant role in gaining credibility for Burson-Marsteller in both business and government circles. Scott, who is fluent in Mandarin, left us in 1998 to join a client, United Technologies, and has returned to Washington. Susan Tomsett, Australian by birth, joined us in Shanghai and transferred to Beijing to head our China operations. Her team of local Chinese and expatriate professionals have made Burson-Marsteller the country's premier international public relations firm.

My first visit to China in 1986 was in response to an invitation from our joint venture partner, Xinhua. Almost 20 years later, that trip ranks among my most memorable experiences. Our "party of four" included my wife, Bette, and my associates Godfrey Scotchbrook and Scott Seligman, both well known to our hosts. During the ten days of our visit – each day meticulously planned hour-by-hour – our escort consisted of a senior Xinhua executive and a mid-level Xinhua journalist, two brand new sedans of Chinese manufacture and two chauffeurs. Since the two Xinhua representatives had the same surname Yu, we referred to them, with their amusement and total endorsement as "Old Mr. Yu" and "Young Mr. Yu." (Scott Seligman was our interpreter.) At the time of our visit, China was at an early stage in developing an infrastructure to accommodate visitors from abroad. That Bette and I were assigned a suite in what was then regarded as

Beijing's most desirable hotel was something extra special. Xinhua's hospitality started with a banquet for about two hundred guests at the Great Hall of the People hosted by its director general. Escorted tours of the Forbidden City, the Great Wall and Beijing's national art museum followed. Of the numerous restaurants we visited, the one that stands out was the "duck factory" where duck combs and duck tongues were among the delicacies.

In Shanghai, we were treated no less royally. The suite assigned to us at the Jinjiang Hotel was the one occupied by President Nixon when he visited Shanghai. We attended a fashion show with svelte Chinese models and spent a delightful evening at the Peace Hotel listening to pop tunes of the 1930s and 1940s played by an aging Chinese combo whose members gave the impression they had played the same songs, uninterrupted, since their introduction before, during and immediately following World War II. One day we drove two hours on a one-lane paved road to Suzhou, frequently referred to as the Venice of China. Next on our itinerary was the ancient Chinese capital Xion, where the recent stunning archaeological discovery, the buried terra-cotta soldiers dating back two millennia, was the principal attraction. The 8,000 life-sized uniformed soldiers and their weaponry and their horses and chariots in parade formation were in pristine condition. A temporary viewing platform, covered by a hastily built shed-like wood structure, had been constructed to accommodate sightseers flocking to Xion to see what globally came to be known as "the terra cotta soldiers" now housed in a structure that covers about five acres.

In expressing my appreciation to Xinhua's director general for the ultra hospitable reception, I told him I was especially touched because the revenues Burson-Marsteller would generate for Xinhua during the next several years would likely be small – in the range of $250,000 to $500,000 annually. To my surprise, he told me that this was a significant sum that came at a timely moment. The fact that the funds were U.S. dollars, then in short supply in a China just emerging as a commercial trading nation, was of great consequence. He planned to use them to augment the hard currency appropriation from the government to speed the computerization of Xinhua around the world. He was also optimistic about China Global Public Relations as a future revenue producer for Xinhua. His optimism was well-placed. China Global is now among the largest domestic public relations firms largely serving, as planned from the outset, Chinese companies marketing their products in mainland China.

The Burson-Marsteller connection with Korea started in the late 1970s when Godfrey Scotchbrook, manager of B-M/Hong Kong, discovered Joanne Lee and her firm, Star Communications, in Seoul. Star Communications became our affiliate, and Joanne became a close friend from the time we first met in New York. She is a lady of beauty, charm and intelligence. In business matters she has few equals.

My personal interest in Korea started when the International Olympic Committee (IOC) awarded Seoul the venue for the 1988 Summer Olympic Games. Since Burson-Marsteller had had a significant role in the 1984 Summer Games in Los Angeles, I was passionately committed to a continuing relationship with the Olympic movement. My objective was to make the Seoul Olympic Organizing Committee (SLOOC) a B-M client.

In the three years before the actual 1988 Olympic Summer Games, I made about ten trips to Seoul and developed a number of high-level relationships both in government and business. One of them was Park Seh-jik, who had succeeded Roh Tae-Woo as SLOOC's director-general shortly after we got on board. General Roh was appointed leader of the reigning Democratic Liberal Party and eventually became the first democratically elected President of the Republic of Korea. The Korean economy surged during the years preceding the Olympics, and I was determined that a legacy of our engagement would be an ongoing Burson-Marsteller office in Seoul. At the time, however, Korean law forbade foreign ownership of advertising agencies. Although the law was not explicit, the ban was thought to cover public relations firms as well. While Star Communications and Joanne Lee were not involved in our Olympics assignment, my intention was for her to have a significant role in the Korean launch of a full-service Burson-Marsteller office.

During the early part of 1988, I informed a couple of well-placed Korean friends of our desire to establish a permanent B-M presence in Korea after our SLOOC assignment. As the year progressed, I had conversations at the Ministry of Culture and Information and the Ministry of Trade, the government entities that had oversight under the law. Both were sympathetic to what I hoped to achieve, but they were non-committal about issuing a permit that would allow us to open an office.

During the week of the Olympics opening ceremony in September, I was told by a person whose authority I had no reason to doubt that if we applied for a permit to open an office in Korea, it would not be denied. I took this to mean that our three-year commitment to making the 1988 Summer Games a runaway success was recognized from "on high" in the Korean government and that the permit was our reward. I learned later that the government had also decided to relax, over a period of several years, the restriction on foreign ownership of advertising agencies. Before the end of the year, we filed our application and it was quickly approved. This action enabled us to acquire Joanne Lee's Star Communications and it became the nucleus of our business in Korea. Over the years we had worked together, Joanne was deeply steeped in the ways of Burson-Marsteller and knew many of our people in U.S., European and Asian offices. In a sense, we were starting a new office with someone we identified with and could call our own.

In the meantime, Bill Rylance and Bryan Matthews – when we dedicated to full time on-site service – after three years of high energy performance that was universally commended by our clients at SLOOC and at the highest levels of government, decided to leave Burson-Marsteller and start their own business. They named it Merit Communications. While I would have preferred that they continue their careers with Burson-Marsteller, their departure was without rancor. I wished them well and continued to maintain my friendship with both of them. For almost ten years, Burson-Marsteller and Merit were competitors in Seoul (it pains me to admit that Merit was the market leader for most of that time). We transferred Jeff Hunt from B-M/New York to serve as chief operating officer for the new B-M/Seoul with principal emphasis on reinforcing Burson-Marsteller culture and methodology. By 1997, after Jeff's transfer to another new office in Mexico City, Joanne Lee decided to reorder her priorities and severely curtailed her involvement with our business. That led to discussions with Bill and Bryan that resulted in our merging B-M/Seoul into Merit. In exchange, Burson-Marsteller became a minority shareholder in Merit with options to acquire the business. Two years later, we acquired 100 percent ownership and Bill Rylance departed Seoul after fourteen years to become Asia/Pacific Regional CEO based in Hong Kong. Today, we are undisputed market leader in Korea.

———— ∞∞∞ ————

Australia was on our "to do" list until the spring of 1980 when our Asian regional manager, Peter Bostock, and I met in Sydney to determine how we would introduce Burson-Marsteller in that faraway market. With a population of about twenty million, Australia has perhaps the highest per capita density of public relations professionals and firms in the world. And like Canada, its population occupies only a small sliver of the country's land mass spread across thousands of miles. The public relations consultancy business in Australia was then dominated by two large firms, our traditional global competitor Hill & Knowlton, which had acquired Eric White & Associates a couple of years earlier, and IPR (International Public Relations), a firm headquartered in Melbourne. In the next tier were six to eight mid-sized firms each with fifteen to thirty employees. And in the third tier were more than a hundred small firms with one to five employees, many home-based. My intuition was to start offices afresh in Australia as we had in Europe. But I thought it would be instructive for Peter Bostock and me to meet with the owner/managers of four of the mid-sized Australian firms that had previously approached me in New York to talk about mergers or otherwise representing Burson-Marsteller. We also met with a half-dozen corporate public relations officers from whom we sought to evaluate our potential in Australia. We were even briefed by the head of Hill & Knowlton's offices.

After a week of discussions that gave us a well-rounded picture of the public relations market in Australia, Bostock and I concluded that Burson-Marsteller would be best served starting its own office. Our reasoning was simple: if we acquired one of the mid-sized firms, we would likely be positioned below the top tier. But if we started our own office, little matter that it would be teeny compared to our two top competitors, our global reputation would position us with the top firms. In July, Peter Walford moved from B-M/Tokyo to Sydney. In August, John Birch, another Brit, went from B-M/London to Melbourne. Requiring representation in Canberra in order to take on public affairs assignments, we joint ventured with Australian PA Consultants and eventually established our own office in Canberra. In 1982, having acquired Bridgestone Tires and Mitsubishi Autos as clients, we opened a small office in Adelaide which, for the years it was in existence, was our most consistently profitable operation in Australia. In 1984, when Paul Adams was transferred after a decade at B-M/Tokyo to B-M/Melbourne to head our Australian operations, we started offices in Brisbane (to capitalize on the high-tech industry that was developing in Queensland as well as the World's Fair in 1993) and in Perth on Australia's west coast (where a petroleum/minerals exploration boomlet was underway). To serve a major information technology client, we opened a small office in Auckland, New Zealand in 1986. Today, we have offices in Sydney and Melbourne, the two major population centers.

From the time we began operations in Asia in 1973, we considered other locations and, for brief periods, operated our own offices in several countries where we do not now have wholly-owned offices. As early as 1976, we began a relationship with George Capps in Bangkok that lasted for two decades, first as an affiliate and, in 1986, when we acquired his business and established a Burson-Marsteller presence. George had been in Thailand as a member of the Peace Corps in the 1960s and was fluent in three Thai dialects. Despite the country's sixty million population, the market for public relations in Thailand has been slow developing and B-M divested the office to local management in 1998. The firm, now a B-M affiliate, is known as Aziam Burson-Marsteller.

In Taiwan, we had an affiliate relationship with United Pacific International Inc. (UPII) dating to the late 1970s. One of the most interesting evenings I ever spent was at the old Grand Hotel in Taipei with Jimmy Li, the father-in-law of one of the owners, a close confidante of Chang Kai-shek. The two of them left mainland China together to go to Taiwan where Li was one of the Generalissimo's most trusted advisers. Jimmy Li headed the Chinese Information Service in Washington during World War II and could recite the batting averages of baseball players of that era in both major leagues. In 1991, we established a joint venture with UPII which was dissolved in 1996.

In Indonesia, we depended on affiliates for two decades to supplement the efforts of B-M/Singapore staff fulfilling client needs in that populous country. With the promise of economic and political stability in 1992, we established PT Burson-Marsteller Indonesia with a staff of six people. By July 1997, the office had a staff of forty and was profitable, its client base mostly U.S. and European multinationals. By year-end, after a major economic downturn in southeast Asia that had a severe impact on Indonesia, the staff was reduced to a handful of people and the office, as such, was closed in 1998. Currently, Indonesia is mainly served from our Singapore office.

In India, the second largest market in Asia – and one with enormous economic potential – we entered into a formal joint venture with Roger Pereira Communications Pvt Ltd. after working with him and his staff in Mumbai (Bombay) for a decade or more. Burson-Marsteller held a minority stock interest, with options to acquire more. For many years, the relationship was productive, but in 2002, a decision was made by B-M management to end it because of the need for more broadly based coverage, both geographically and functionally. Burson-Marsteller is now represented in India by Genesis, a firm of more than a hundred people with offices in five major cities. We have high hopes that India, like China, will one day be among the largest markets for public relations and public affairs services.

⊖⊗⊗⊖

Burson-Marsteller has been in Asia thirty years, in Australia twenty-three years. The region accounts for about fifteen percent of our total revenues. For many years, it was our fastest growing region percentage-wise but the late 1990s were not kind to either our business or to the region's economy in general. Growth resumed in the new century and the chances are good that Asia/Pacific will again grow dramatically in coming years. Given political stability and a recovering world economy, Asia has the potential once again to live up to its promise. It's hard to overlook that two countries in the region have the world's largest populations – each of them an awakening giant economically with the potential of substantial future rewards. Taking Burson-Marsteller to Asia in the early 1970s was one of my best decisions.

Chapter 7

The Americas: The United States, Canada, Latin America

E ven while immersed in establishing Burson-Marsteller in Europe and Asia and making several two- to three-week visits to the two continents every year for thirty years, I always knew that the "growth engine" for our business was the United States. From the time we dared think we had the potential to become a global business, I assumed that our primary revenue source would be U.S.-headquartered multinational corporations. Accordingly, I pursued the goal of making Burson-Marsteller a differentiated market leader capable of attracting global clients in our home market.

Fortunately for me, I was supported by a management team that shared my vision and had the ability to orchestrate the most dramatic expansion of a public relations firm in history. Literally scores of B-M colleagues in the U.S. contributed at one time or another at one or more geographical locations. I have tried to make the point that many, many people have dedicated themselves to the making of Burson-Marsteller. I also had Bill Marsteller's support and the support of Marsteller Advertising and people like Richard C. (Dick) Christian, Lou Magnani, Ray Gaulke, Bruce Cole, Art Cowles, Bruce Richardson, Bob Trebus, Milton Sutton and others who helped sell public relations to their U.S. advertising clients.

By 1965, we had offices in New York, Chicago and Pittsburgh, in Toronto and in Geneva and Brussels. Our total revenues were $1,328,000 (about ten million in 2003 dollars) and we were intent on adding new clients and more business from existing clients. We were largely business-to-business and widely rated the top agency for industrial accounts. We also had experience in corporate/financial relations, a result of our work for Rockwell and Clark Equipment. As the decade of the 1960s came to an end, our three offices in the U.S. could each point to impressive additions to our client list.

∽∞∾

B-M/New York, always our largest office, set the pace. Two big wins in the early 1960s were Armco Steel, the nation's fourth largest steel company, and Babcock & Wilcox, the largest maker of boilers for electric utilities and a major factor in nuclear reactors. In the late-1960s good work by B-M/Geneva helped make Texas Instruments a U.S. client and Johnson & Johnson gave us our first assignment. But the "win of the decade" was Owens-Corning Fiberglas (OCF), a client that provided both a large budget and many opportunities to produce outstanding programs which brought us acclaim and esteem. Winning OCF was another of our defining moments.

It was during the 1970s when my associates and I first realized we were on the way to becoming the world's largest public relations firm. B-M/New York was the brightest star in the Burson Marsteller firmament. (In 1971, B-M ranked third behind Hill & Knowlton and Ruder·Finn; we moved up a notch in 1972 and remained there a full decade; in 1983 we topped the list.) Our growth rate was consistently the highest among the larger firms as new business from blue chip clients poured in. General Motors gave us a great lift in 1970 when we were chosen to be its corporate public relations counsel (more about that in a later installment). Merrill Lynch and Burger King, then our largest consumer client, signed on in the mid-1970s along with Johnson & Johnson's Tylenol. Other major wins included United Technologies, Chemical Bank, Piper Aircraft, American Dental Association, Hoffmann-LaRoche, American Bankers Association, Gillette, Gerber (baby foods), American Express and Dow Chemical. In 1979, B-M/NY serviced our three largest clients: Burger King, Owens-Corning and Merrill Lynch.

We moved our original B-M/NY office to larger space in the New York Daily News Building (220 East 42nd Street) a year after we opened for business. We moved again in early 1955 when Marsteller Advertising added a third office in

New York. After a year on their board, I persuaded Bill Marsteller that a New York office was essential to the growth of the advertising business. Marsteller Advertising acquired a mid-size industrial agency called Rickard & Company with enough space in a second-rate building at 11 East 36th Street to house B-M/NY. Although our people were less than happy about the step-down in accommodations, they knew it was temporary and almost immediately added Rickard clients Ingersoll-Rand, Cincinnati Milling Machine and Metal & Thermit (an industrial division of American Can) to our list. In July 1958, Burson-Marsteller and Marsteller Advertising moved to a new building at 800 Second Avenue, diagonally across the street from our former Daily News location. Four years later we added a second floor (B-M on one, Marsteller Advertising on the other, the pattern we followed in cities where we both had offices). In 1967, the two businesses signed up for four floors, about forty-five thousand square feet, in another new building at 866 Third Avenue (between 52/53 Streets) with a twenty-year lease and an option to add a fifth floor in five years at $6 a square foot. B-M/New York's growth surge started soon after and continued for two decades. We leased three additional eleven thousand square foot floors at 866 Third Avenue (at up to $37.50 a square foot) and were forced to lease floors in three other buildings – 888 Third Avenue, 919 Third Avenue and 757 Third Avenue. We operated in that mode for five years until we moved Burson-Marsteller to 230 Park Avenue South in January 1986 – six hundred and fifty-three people made the move. No public relations firm today has that many people in a single location.

The growth of our client list in the 1980s continued unabated. While B-M/NY competed vigorously against other firms many new accounts came to us either unsolicited or without competition. Among the latter were Coca-Cola, DuPont and GE Appliances. After "courting" AT&T for almost ten years, in 1983 we competed for their Los Angeles Olympic Torch Run project and won the business. The Torch Run remains the largest single project ever undertaken by Burson-Marsteller. For more than a decade AT&T was a major B-M client. Another significant addition was Philip Morris in 1987. We got the business without competition or even a formal presentation. Among other major clients gained by B-M/NY in the 1980s were Digital Equipment (DEC), M&M/Mars, Met Life, Pfizer, Glaxo, Sandoz, the Committee for Energy Awareness (a well-funded initiative to promote energy conservation and energy-producing options), Tropicana and the U.S. Army (recruiting program) and the U.S. Postal Service, the latter two in tandem with Young & Rubicam. A new management at Burger King terminated both us and its advertising agency (J. Walter Thompson) and we quickly joined forces with Wendy's.

While growth slowed in the 1990s, B-M/NY added new clients like Andersen Consulting (now Accenture). Our former client Jim Murphy, who joined us after five years at Merrill Lynch, led our presentation to the then newly formed Arthur Andersen & Co. business unit. Two years later he was hired by Andersen Consulting as chief marketing officer. Accenture has been one of B-M's top five clients ever since. Our work for IBM ballooned during the early years of the decade and we took on major strategic assignments for Ontario Hydro and Quebec Hydro while increasing substantially our business from Citicorp, Warner Lambert and American Home Products (now Wyeth).

During our 50-year history, B-M/New York has accounted for approximately twenty-five percent of the company's total global revenues and a comparable portion of profits. Almost all that growth was organic, from existing clients and new business. There has been only one acquisition in New York – Theodore Sills & Company in 1970. It came about because I thought it would jump-start our consumer marketing capability. Ted Sills built a unique business – the largest public relations firm specializing in food products. He started his business after World War II in Chicago, but eighty percent of revenues came from his thirty-person New York office, all female with the exception of the mail room attendant. Sills lived in Los Angeles where he had a small office. The only other male in the company was the Chicago manager, John Bohan. Sills deliberately structured his business in a way that enabled him to play golf year-round in a location where he wanted to retire. He and his wife Anna Laurie lived in Pacific Palisades across the street from the future governor of California and future president of the United States – Ronald Reagan.

At age sixty Sills acted on a plan to perpetuate his business and convert his equity into funds for retirement. I was aware of his firm for several years because of its unique reputation as a food specialist. His plan called for selling his business, working five years and retiring at sixty-five. It took us only a few weeks to reach agreement – we gave him $500,000 in stock to be repurchased by the company at the then book value when he retired. Actually, he remained until he was sixty-eight and his stock was worth about two million dollars. We added more than a dozen first-rate consumer marketing professionals. Sills clients included the National Pasta Association, Church & Dwight (Arm & Hammer baking soda), Spanish green olives, Crisco (Procter & Gamble), Pickle Packers Association and California state-financed marketing programs for artichokes, apricots and strawberries.

B-M/NY became the largest public relations office in New York in the early 1980s and held that position until 2001. For two decades it housed the world's largest collection of public relations professionals at one location.

Shortly before his death in 2000, George Lazarus, *The Chicago Tribune* advertising/marketing columnist and my friend for thirty years, asked me whether I kept count of my visits to Chicago. Although I didn't, it took me only a few seconds to respond "five hundred." George's seemingly logical reaction was "how can that be possible?" I explained "I visited Chicago at least once a month for more than forty years – forty times twelve is four hundred-and-eighty and I feel secure rounding it up to five hundred." B-M/Chicago is my most-visited office and B-M/Washington is a close second.

When the original Chicago Park Hyatt near the Water Tower, a jewel of a hotel, was razed six years ago, I received a package that contained a brass plate mounted on a walnut base bearing the etched words "Ten Hundred." With it was a note from the manager telling me that, as one of the hotel's most frequent guests, he was enclosing a souvenir from the suite I had occupied so often during the quarter century the original Park Hyatt was in existence. (For the record: while I usually occupied a suite when visiting Chicago, I never paid the suite rate. Because of my frequent visits and the patronage of our Chicago office for client and office events, my reservation at the Park Hyatt was invariably upgraded and suite Ten Hundred was my favorite.)

My frequent visits to Chicago started even before Burson-Marsteller was legally incorporated. In fact, my first non-client priority when B-M opened for business on March 2, 1953, was a Chicago office. Although long-term I was committed to building a B-M client list independent of Marsteller Advertising, I recognized that our hottest immediate prospects were Marsteller Advertising clients. In addition to an aggressive new business effort, we had to establish a capability in Chicago to handle marketing publicity for our big client Clark Equipment (I personally handled Clark at the corporate level). For the first five years of our existence, I was in our Chicago office every two to three weeks for stays of at least two days.

The first person hired for B-M/Chicago was Bob Hartney, a recent graduate of the School of Journalism at the University of Illinois (Bill Marsteller's alma mater). Hartney was a capable writer who looked mature for an entry level account person.

He showed promise from the outset, stayed at B-M/Chicago five years, then transferred to B-M/New York where he remained almost ten years before joining our client Oak Industries and moving to southern California. Our second hire was Aubrey Cookman, a well-known Chicago news reporter and a retired Air Force colonel. Cookman, whom Bill Marsteller had known for many years, was general manager. Although he had managed an Air Force public information unit, Cookman had never worked for a public relations firm. He headed the office six years and left to join our client Universal Oil Products. We then had a staff of twelve.

The part I liked most about those early visits to Chicago was my interaction with George Spatta, Clark Equipment CEO, with whom I had dinner or lunch almost every visit, some times at Clark headquarters in Buchanan, Michigan, a hundred miles east of Chicago (he always sent his chauffeur to transport me). I also spent a lot of time selling public relations services to Marsteller Advertising clients, mainly medium-sized industrial companies like Calumet & Hecla (copper mining), Century Electric (electric motors), National-Standard (steel springs) and Roura Iron Works (heavy mining equipment). We had a fairly good success rate building a client list that enabled us to add staff. As in New York, we preferred hiring journalists with industry know-how, many of them graduate engineers who were trade paper reporters and editors.

During the next ten years, B-M/Chicago began to be recognized as a presence in the Chicago public relations community. Its client list in the 1960s boasted a number of prominent Midwest companies: A. B. Dick, whose name was synonymous with the now-outdated "Mimeograph" machine; Johnson Service, climate control specialists; Abbott Laboratories, pharmaceuticals; John Sexton, one of the largest institutional food service companies, and the Railway Progress Institute, an organization set up to support government funding to maintain rail service. For almost a quarter century, B-M/Chicago's largest client was Clark Equipment served by an account team that ranged from four to six professionals, some totally dedicated to Clark.

Although B-M/Chicago was growing profitably and we had hired good people, the early management of the office was erratic. Believing that a strong operation in Chicago was critical to our future success, in the early 1970s I asked Jim Dowling to go to Chicago as general manager. Jim, at the time was B-M/New York's general manager and a move to Chicago would seem to be a step downward. But he, too, recognized the importance of that office to the overall success of Burson-Marsteller and he and his wife, Anne, gave up a newly-purchased home in New Canaan to move to Chicago's northern suburbs.

An important addition to the client list was Beatrice Foods, which provided an opportunity to implement a number of highly visible initiatives, including staging and sponsoring the first Chicago Marathon. Until it was acquired in a leveraged buyout by KKR, Beatrice was B-M/Chicago's largest client. Other significant account gains of that era included Sears, *The Chicago Tribune*, G.D. Searle (pharmaceuticals), Trans-Union Corporation (leased railroad tank cars and credit information).

John La Sage was appointed B-M/Chicago general manager in 1978 and has been a senior presence in the Chicago area ever since. He has been active in numerous city and state civic and cultural initiatives and has been well-known in the upper echelons of the Chicago business community. John played a major role in winning the McDonald's business and in landing other major clients like Sears, Ameritech, S. C. Johnson, Spiegel, Gatorade, NutraSweet, Dow Corning and Miller Beer.

For almost a decade, starting in the 1980s B-M/Chicago held the number one position in *Crain's Chicago Business* ranking of public relations firms.

B-M/Pittsburgh, established in 1957, was another office I visited frequently during our first quarter century. For more than twenty years Rockwell was among our top five clients and I was in Pittsburgh every month. CEO Willard F. (Al) Rockwell took a hands-on role in the public relations program and B-M/Pittsburgh also worked for several Rockwell business units. On a smaller scale in a much smaller market, B-M/Pittsburgh, like B-M/Chicago, was also growing. Its early clients included Koppers, manufacturers of coke and coal tar products; Pittsburgh-Corning, the largest glass block manufacturer; a law firm, a manufacturer of steel mill rolling equipment and L. B. Foster Company, the nation's largest distributor of rail, sheet steel piling and pipe and other tubular products (a company then owned by my wife's family).

In future years, even as some *FORTUNE* 500 corporations moved from Pittsburgh to other locations, the B-M/Pittsburgh client list included the area's best known names – Westinghouse, U.S. Steel, Duquesne Light, Mellon Bank, Allegheny Ludlum, Pittsburgh National Bank (PNB), Wheeling Pittsburgh, Calgon and Bayer. Gulf (gasoline), a major client for a decade, was acquired by Chevron. In the early 1980s, after Y&R acquired us, Marsteller Advertising management decided their Pittsburgh office was "no longer strategic" to the business.

B-M/Pittsburgh annexed the local Marsteller operation, putting Burson-Marsteller in the advertising business and setting the stage for the relaunch of Marsteller Advertising as a B-M practice area.

B-M/Pittsburgh is as well known, as well established and as well regarded in its hometown as any office in the B-M system. While this has been the case for many years, participation in civic and community initiatives intensified in the mid-1980s when Sheila Rathke, now an executive at the University of Pittsburgh, and her successor and present incumbent, Laura Gongos, took over the general manager role. The office is widely known for its much-anticipated annual "Hair of the Dog" party – described by one publication as "the hottest ticket in town." It started in 1962 (the equivalent of almost 300 "dog" years!) to express appreciation to the Pittsburgh press corps, print and electronic, as well as clients. The name derives from the timing of the event, the week following New Year's Eve. Once a small intimate event, nowadays more than two hundred guests attend.

We staked our west coast foothold in California in 1966 by sending B-M/Pittsburgh's Jim Foy to Los Angeles. It became our fourth U.S. office and enabled us to claim we were "national" in scope. The business was slow taking off and Foy resigned to become one of LA's most popular news commentators during the 1970s and 1980s. Al Smith, who was among the first dozen account executives we hired in New York, succeeded Foy as general manager. He quickly built a small but solid corporate/financial business by landing clients like MCA, the owner of Universal Studios and the largest producer of TV shows; Ticor, the nation's largest title insurance company; the then publicly-listed Coca-Cola of Los Angeles, Coke's Southern California franchisee; Ralph's, the big supermarket chain; and Bekins, the largest moving company.

Los Angeles – actually all of California – has been a difficult market for national public relations firms. Few have been consistently successful over a sustained time frame. One reason for our failing to reach our objectives, I believe, is that we have lacked "a California strategy" that treated the state as a discrete market. We also failed to recognize the idiosyncratic nature of the market – unlike our behavior in overseas markets. (Experience tells me that California should be treated the way we treat overseas markets; it's that different from others in the U.S. and, as the fifth or sixth largest economy in the world, it's big enough!)

When Al Smith returned to B-M/New York in 1983, we acquired Wolcott & Company, a firm headed by a native Californian well regarded as a past president of the Public Relations Society of America and for representing the New York World's Fair in the mid-1960s. Three years earlier (1980), we had established an office in San Francisco, following our acquisition by Young & Rubicam and its introductions to Chevron and Gallo Wines, both major Y&R clients. B-M/San Francisco also had Levi Strauss as a client.

The "high tech" boom started in the early 1980s and its epicenter was Silicon Valley. We transferred Tom Nunan, an electrical engineer high-techie at B-M/Chicago, to manage B-M/Los Angeles. While we were outgrowing our original image as a b-to-b "industrial" agency, we already had a dozen clients in the rapidly growing high-tech/electronics industry. For about five years, Burson-Marsteller staged an annual breakfast at the industry's big Comdex trade show in Las Vegas that was well attended by the electronics trade press. In 1982, we hired a well-connected high-tech professional with an entrepreneurial flair named Rene White and opened an office in Silicon Valley (Santa Clara). In a couple years, Rene acquired enough clients, some of them under-financed start-ups, to require more than fifty staff people. Rene was then transferred to New York to head up what we hoped would be a U.S. technology practice, the impetus being the dramatic growth along Route 128 in the Boston area as well as the burgeoning technology community in Virginia and Maryland adjacent to Washington. (Texas Instruments, then at its peak as an industry leader, was a client, and for several years the largest B-M/Los Angeles client was Epson, then the biggest name in printers.) Moving Rene White was a mistake. We lost our way in Silicon Valley and failed to penetrate the high tech community on the east coast. In 1987, we consolidated the remains of our Silicon Valley business into B-M/San Francisco after taking a bad debt write-off of $2 million. In the interim, we opened a small high-tech office in Orange County in 1984 and closed it a year later.

In retrospect, we (I) never made the connection between the "high-tech" that took off in the last two decades of the twentieth century with the "low-tech" that we had mastered thirty years earlier. We were once extremely good at hiring mechanical, electrical and civil engineers who were both capable journalists and effective publicists and selling their services to technically-oriented clients. We were not nearly as aggressive in bringing on engineers or otherwise technically trained writer/publicists competent in the new age of cybernetics, fiber optics and other technologies within the high-tech rubric. We simply failed to foresee early enough the potential of high tech as a large specialized business.

We returned to Silicon Valley in 1997 with a Palo Alto office that principally served Sun Microsystems, then our largest technology client. Two years later, with the profusion of new dot.com clients, we consolidated Palo Alto with B-M/San Francisco. At the peak of the boom, we had about 120 dot.com clients (unlike the earlier wave of high tech start-ups, they paid their bills!). The downside of the boom was that we lost valued staff professionals to dot.com employers on an average of more than one a week, all tempted by now worthless options. The fall-out when the bubble burst was severe for B-M/San Francisco – about thirty people remained from a staff that once numbered one hundred and fifty – but the direct effect on other B-M offices was minimal. B-M San Francisco's present staff is now about fifty after winning H-P as a client. In 1999, we opened a small office in San Diego to service Qualcomm, another major high-tech client. Lincoln-Mercury and Sony have also been served by B-M/San Diego.

While we missed out on becoming the undisputed leader in the high-tech industry – our position in the low-tech era – we have since aggregated a highly qualified staff that provides in depth services globally to some of the most impressive names in the high tech pantheon, among them SAP and H-P (Hewlett-Packard), both clients in a dozen or more countries, as well as Qualcomm and Alcatel. In years past, we have had major relationships with IBM, Sun Microsystems, Digital Equipment (DEC), Nortel, Apple, most of the regional Bells and numerous overseas telecoms.

We were late recognizing the public affairs potential that California offers. In 1992, a full quarter century after going to Los Angeles, we opened an office in Sacramento and during the past decade have effectively handled a broad array of public issues, some highly visible and highly contentious like deregulation of electric utilities. At present, one of our most critical assignments involves protection of intellectual property rights for the Recording Industry Association of America. Water issues have also been prominent on the B-M/Sacramento agenda.

Our current strong presence in Washington is a Jim Dowling legacy. In its early years, the B-M/Washington staff ranged from twenty to thirty employees. A cyclical operation with marginal profitability, its business came largely from referrals by other B-M offices. Its work consisted mainly of providing public relations support, working with the media, and handling legislative issues that affected clients of other U.S. offices. We entered the market in 1968 by acquiring a six-person business owned by Carl Levin, a former correspondent for the *New York Herald-Tribune* whose principal clients were Schenley Industries (whiskey) and Abbott Laboratories (pharmaceuticals). Two B-M clients – Asea, the large Swedish electrical equipment manufacturer, and Armco Steel – required Washington assistance on trade issues and soon became clients of our new office.

Dowling felt that Burson-Marsteller would never be a major factor on the Washington scene unless we broadened services to include a legislative/lobbying component. For several years, we hired highly qualified legislative specialists with good experience on Capitol Hill or in the executive branch of government as an extension of our public relations service. While they did good work for clients, Burson-Marsteller was seldom a contender for major Washington assignments. This changed rapidly after Dowling hired Tom Bell, a well-credentialed Washington hand who was president of the Hudson Institute, a policy think tank headquartered in Indianapolis. Earlier, Bell was chief of staff to Senator William E. Brock and a staffer in the Nixon White House. Bell hired an impressive lobbying staff that represented both political parties, but he came to the realization that Burson-Marsteller's strong identity as the world's largest public relations firm was not necessarily a plus factor in selling legislative support (lobbying) services.

Within a three month-period in 1990-91, Burson-Marsteller acquired two well-regarded lobbying firms. The first was Gold & Liebengood, a firm of twenty whose principals, Martin Gold and Howard Liebengood, had been long-time associates of Senate Majority Leader Howard Baker. The other was Black Manaford Stone & Kelly, one of Washington's highest profile lobbying firms headed by Charles Black, a well-placed political adviser to both Presidents Ronald Reagan and George W.H. Bush. Peter Kelly was a former finance chairman of the Democratic party. Its staff numbered more than fifty, many, like Jim Healy, House Ways and Means Committee chief of staff for Chairman Daniel Rostenkowski, and Scott Pastrick, former treasurer of the Democratic National Committee. By 1994, Burson-Marsteller and its wholly-owned legislative subsidiaries became Washington's largest public relations/lobbying firm with one hundred and fifty employees. Since then, the lobbying arm has renamed itself BKSH and expanded into Europe with an office in Brussels that works with the European Community and an office in Berlin.

In 1997, B-M/Washington joined forces with a gem of a firm specializing in constituency and "grass root" relations called The Direct Impact Company, now a wholly-owned Burson-Marsteller subsidiary. The firm has a field force of 1,200 on-call bi-partisan representatives in all fifty states qualified to deliver client messages to legislators and other public officials as well as reporters and editors at both print and electronic media. Started by John Brady, who recently retired from the business, Direct Impact is now headed by Craig Veith, former head of B-M's Media Relations Practice.

B-M/Washington has taken a leading role in numerous high profile issues covering a broad range of the political spectrum. A major client for three years in the 1990s was the Government of Mexico prior to passage of the North American Free Trade Agreement by the U.S. Congress. The office has worked on numerous trade and tax issues through the years and is currently supporting the Canadian forest products industry to reduce the tariff on lumber imports from Canada. Its longest-lasting relationship was with the asbestos industry, an association that continued for thirty years.

In 1996, B-M/Washington was hired by the Department of the Treasury to introduce redesigned paper currency in $5/$10/$20/$50/$100 denominations. A large part of the effort was in countries of the former Soviet Union, where a significant amount of the larger denominated U.S. bills are held. The office was chosen again in 2002 by the Treasury Department to implement a similar program for further design changes in the $20/$50/$100 bills.

After Coca-Cola became a client in 1983, we needed an office in Atlanta to work on Coke marketing programs. Although Atlanta was at the center of one of the nation's fastest growing regional economies, I had not seriously thought about opening an office there (despite my Southern roots!). Retrospectively, I suspect I was, in a geographical sense, otherwise preoccupied. Bob Cohn, co-owner/founder of Atlanta's "hottest" public relations firm, got word to me that he wanted to merge his firm into Burson-Marsteller On my next visit to Atlanta I met Cohn, a gregarious, larger-than-life creative powerhouse. His partner, Norman Wolfe, was a perfect offset for his strong personality – soft-spoken, thoughtful, attentive-to-detail. C&W's mostly youngish staff of about twenty-five included a publicity genius named Bob Hope, who distinguished himself publicizing Ted Turner's Atlanta Braves baseball team. Almost forgotten now, he fathered the idea of a wet T-shirt contest to boost attendance at Braves games. Hope later transferred to B-M/New York and within a three-year period took a leading role helping B-M clients land franchises for the Miami Marlins and Colorado Rockies (baseball), Charlotte Hornets (basketball) and Ottawa Senators (hockey).

We acquired Cohn & Wolfe in a stock-for-stock transaction effective January 1984. I suspect it was our most successful acquisition. In 1983, Cohn & Wolfe's income was barely $1.5 million. After the turn of the century, fee income exceeded $50 million. When we acquired the business, C&W/Atlanta produced more than eighty percent of its revenues. As part of a southeast regional strategy, it had small outposts in Charlotte, Nashville and Tampa, which we closed during the next twelve months or so. Integrating the marketing portion of our new Coca-Cola business was easy because Cohn & Wolfe had already successfully carried out numerous Coke projects (and I had talked about Cohn & Wolfe with Coca-Cola management before finalizing the acquisition).

Though our original intention was to change the Cohn & Wolfe name to Burson-Marsteller (after using a dual name for a respectable period of time), Jim Dowling and I decided (wisely it turned out!) to retain the Cohn & Wolfe nomenclature and operate the firm as a B-M subsidiary. There were several reasons for the decision. One was Cohn & Wolfe's strong identity in Atlanta and throughout the southeast as a creative hot shop also strong in sports promotion. We were concerned this positioning would be lost if we integrated C&W into B-M. A second reason was our perceived need for a "second network" to handle conflicts and clients whose budgets were thought insufficient to assure attention from rapidly-growing B-M/New York. The result was that we quickly established a C&W/New York office at a different location. We made clear from the outset that Burson-Marsteller and Cohn & Wolfe would operate independently of one another and we reported the two firms' incomes separately. We were determined to establish truly distinct identities for the two businesses.

The original C&W/New York staff was largely an amalgam of transfers from B-M/NY and C&W/Atlanta, about fifteen in total. The new office grew rapidly as it added its own clients and harvested clients transferred or referred by Burson-Marsteller. In a short time frame, about three years, C&W/New York surpassed C&W/Atlanta in size. Several new C&W offices – Chicago, Milan, Washington, Los Angeles – started with clients that Burson-Marsteller could not, usually for conflict reasons, handle. Cohn & Wolfe reported to the CEO of Burson-Marsteller until 1996 when it began reporting directly to the CEO of Young & Rubicam. Cohn & Wolfe had reached a size where it made sense for it to be a stand-alone entity and B-M and C&W were some times competing against one another for business. Had we combined the income of the two firms, Burson-Marsteller would have been the first public relations firm to reach $300 million in income. (We were the first to reach $100 million and the first to reach $200 million.)

We opened our first Texas office in Houston in 1980. We were responding to the domestic oil and gas boom following the two severe gasoline shortages in 1973 and 1978. Houston was America's fastest growing metropolis and we wanted to be the first large public relations firm to enter the market. We had clients that supplied products and services to what is now known as the energy industry and we knew the oil and gas media well. Fred Thompson transferred from B-M/New York to Houston to start the office and struggled selling and holding on to enough business to maintain a staff of fewer than ten. A principal obstacle was that prospective clients challenged our "high hourly rates" compared with local firms. Among the significant (but small budget) clients were J. Ray McDermott (builder of offshore drilling platforms), Armco's National Tube Division and Baroid (oil well drilling mud).

In 1984, B-M/Chicago landed the city of Fort Worth as a client – our job was to persuade corporations to locate in Fort Worth. The annual budget, funded by the wealthy Bass family, was big for that era (a million dollars). To get the business, a two-year contract, we agreed to set up a service office in Fort Worth. It had four people and landed additional Bass-related business, including the two new, near-empty office towers where we had space rent-free. In fact, we became part of the building's marketing organization. We were phenomenally successful developing interest in Fort Worth – Radio Shack and the U.S. Postal Service were the first to commit to major facilities. We were so successful it was not necessary to continue the program after two years. In the meantime, we opened a small office in Dallas in 1985. A steep decline in crude oil prices caused us to rethink our need for three offices in Texas. In 1986, Read Poland, then the largest public relations firm in Texas, hired most of our people in return for transferring our remaining Texas clients to them. For more than a decade Read Poland was our affiliate in Texas. In 1997, after winning a three-year contract from a state agency to prepare Texans for electric utility deregulation, we returned to Texas with offices in Dallas and Austin under the leadership of Mike Lake, who transferred from B-M/Washington.

As consumer marketing clients jumped on our bandwagon in the early 1980s and our new healthcare practice started its rapid growth, we implemented a strategy to put Burson-Marsteller offices in the top 20 markets in the United States

While we believed these offices – likely to be small, up to a dozen people – would attract significant local clients like the area's public utility or local/ regional bank, the principal reason for them was to establish relationships with local media, both print and electronic. Our premise was that consumer and healthcare, especially pharmaceutical, clients would be best served with strong on-the-scene media relations representatives in their largest markets.

In 1982, Alan Hilberg transferred from B-M/New York to open B-M/ Cleveland, Lew Keim, a long-time B-Mer from B-M/Pittsburgh to B-M/Denver and Ken Trantowski from B-M/Chicago to B-M/Detroit. The choice of those three cities was not random. Our client Wendy's was headquartered in Columbus, Ohio, and we thought it could be better served from Cleveland where we also had TRW as a client. Denver was in the midst of an energy boom and lots of IPO business seemed possible. And we thought an office in Detroit would put us in a better position to attract Ford business. In 1986, we closed Cleveland and Detroit, and, a year later, Denver. We did not attract much desirable local business (we were more expensive than our local competitors) and larger clients in those regions preferred doing business with our larger offices, usually B-M/New York or B-M/Chicago. On the few occasions local office managers were able to get a serious hearing from a nearby *FORTUNE* 500 company, it often conflicted with an existing client. And as technology developed, especially relative to electronic media, we found we did not need a local office to place articles and arrange interviews.

On an "as-needed" basis we have set up a few small local offices to interface with clients. In 1997, transferring Lori Forte Harnick from B-M/NY, we returned to Detroit to service our Lincoln-Mercury business and handle other Ford assignments as well as other clients in the area. In 1999, we established a small office in Harrisburg, Pa., spearheaded by Pat Ford of B-M/Washington to handle what is generally cited as the most effective electric utility deregulation program in the U.S. Lynn Lawson continues to support Pat in that office.

Canada was a challenge for us almost from the time we arrived in 1960 with our fourth office and our first outside the United States. B-M/Toronto remained static in size for almost two decades. Its staff ebbed and flowed from eight to sixteen people and the business was never more than marginally profitable.

Despite a succession of general managers who fell short in building a business,

I continued to think the Canadian market had potential. At the end of 1979, Michael (Mike) Horton, who joined us in Brussels in the late 1960s, completed a three-year assignment in Buenos Aires. I asked him to take on B-M/Toronto and make Burson-Marsteller a major player in Canada. In less than a year, he opened an office in Montreal to serve Canada's French-speaking population, followed by another in Vancouver giving us coast-to-coast coverage, then the only firm that could make that claim. In 1988, we acquired a public affairs firm in Ottawa. After a quarter century in the market, Burson-Marsteller was suddenly Canada's leading public relations/public affairs firm. Our revenues in 1991 exceeded $5 million and pretax profits were more than a million. Our clients included Air Canada, Canadian Post Office, Royal Bank of Canada, British Columbia Forest Products Alliance, Unilever, DuPont and other multinationals. Our board chairman in Canada was Alan Gottlieb, former Canadian ambassador to the United States, and he played a significant role in building our business. Unfortunately, Horton's transfer to head B-M/London in the mid-1980s left us with significant management problems and declining revenues and profits. In 1995, we merged our business in Toronto, Montreal and Ottawa into National Public Relations and B-M/Vancouver became a National office. Founded in 1976 by Luc Beauregard, who remains active in the business, National is now Canada's largest public relations firm. Burson-Marsteller has a twenty-two percent equity interest in National.

———— ❦ ————

We started exploring Latin American as a market in the mid-1960s when client Clark Equipment formed joint ventures in Mexico and Brazil to make automobile and truck transmissions. Robert Benjamin, former *Time* correspondent who pioneered public relations in Mexico in the early 1950s was the nation's leading counselor. He visited me several times in New York and wanted us to acquire his firm. I had other priorities (like making our Geneva office profitable) and misgivings about our immediate prospects in Mexico. Although several clients spoke to me about Mexico, few were actually investing in the market. Instead of an acquisition, I agreed to an affiliate arrangement with Benjamin that endured for more than twenty years. As the Mexican economy grew and the North American Free Trade Agreement (NAFTA) became a reality, we needed a full-fledged Burson-Marsteller office in Mexico City. We acquired a small, well-connected local firm to give us entrée in government circles in 1989, but our real entry into the market was in 1992 when Jeff Hunt, who had headed B-M/Seoul, became our first general manager in Mexico City. Today we are among the larger public relations firms in Mexico.

Burson-Marsteller's first office in South America dates back to December 1976 when we opened in São Paulo, Brazil. It evolved from an affiliation with a small local advertising/public relations firm whose capabilities and service fell short of what our clients required. Paul Adams transferred from B-M/Tokyo to head the office. My first visit to Brazil in 1964 was to get a first-hand "feel" for the market and my stay lasted barely twenty-four hours, aborted by a one-day revolution that unseated the president. Our concerned host suggested that my wife Bette and I flee the country on the first available Pan Am flight after spending only one night at the Copacabana Beach Hotel in Rio de Janeiro. Twelve years later, we launched B-M/São Paulo. Paul Pasternak, B-M/New York, succeeded Paul Adams, whose next assignment was B-M/Melbourne. The first Brazilian national to manage the office was Luis Carlos Andrade, who held that position for more than a decade. During that time, Burson-Marsteller, the first U.S. public relations firm to open an office in South America, vied for the number one position in Brazil with a staff of about sixty.

Our second Latin American office, B-M/San Juan (Puerto Rico) opened in January 1981. As in Oslo, a public relations capability came with an agency Young & Rubicam acquired to establish its foothold in that market. It made sense for Burson-Marsteller to take it over and expand its client base beyond Y&R advertising clients. Serving a limited market, B-M/San Juan has on numerous occasions served the role of a valued "designated" hitter – effectively handling numerous major problems for important U.S. clients.

While we had a U.S. strategy, a European strategy, an Asian strategy and, eventually, even a Canadian strategy, we did not develop a Latin American strategy until the late 1980s when we acquired a small Miami firm in 1988 that had strong Hispanic ties. Called The Marketing Mix (whose name we quickly changed to Burson-Marsteller) and headed by Eileen Marcus (one of the two owners who remained) it did excellent work and we began infiltrating B-M people (recruiting from other offices for Miami was a breeze!). We also concluded that B-M/Miami should be the center of a Latin American region. Its function would be to oversee and coordinate regional accounts and offices (Many *FORTUNE* 500 Latin American regional headquarters are in Miami.) Rissig Licha, who headed B-M/San Juan, went to B-M/Miami as regional market leader with a mandate to expand our operations to other countries in South and Central America as the need for our services arose. He was succeeded in 1993 by Jeff Hunt, who returned to the U.S. after assignments at B-M/Seoul and B-M/Mexico City.

The following year, 1994, was a banner year for B-M's newest region with office openings in Santiago (Chile) in July, Caracas (Venezuela) in August, Buenos Aires (Argentina) in September and Bogotá (Colombia) in November. Ramiro Prudencia, who had been at B-M/Washington three years, became general manager of B-M/Santiago (he now heads B-M/São Paulo). Roy Caple-Hernandez headed B-M/Caracas. Guido Minerva and Michelle Foster were co-leaders of B-M/Buenos Aires until we merged the office with Strategia S.A. and Claudia Gioia became market leader, a position she continues to fill. Michelle Foster moved from Buenos Aires to head B-M/Bogotá, which opened at the time a Y&R office was established in Colombia.

Meanwhile, B-M/Miami not only served as headquarters for Burson-Marsteller business, it also developed a substantial local business. Florida was another triumph for Jim Dowling. After his service as chief executive officer, Jim was given responsibility for the LatAm region in January 1996. In the two years prior to his retirement at the end of 1997, he unified the eight somewhat disparate offices into what is now recognized as the region's premier network. Santiago Hinojosa now heads the Latin American region.

⊗∞⊗

My purpose here has been to document how each of our offices came into being – how, over the past half century, Burson-Marsteller became a global enterprise – fifty-plus offices in thirty-five countries on five continents.

Although we sometimes stumbled and bumbled along the way, Burson-Marsteller today is a fulfillment of a vision that started with our commitment to a European presence forty years ago – a vision that foresaw the growth of a global economy that would require public relations/public affairs services as a natural concomitant of doing business.

While I take pride in creating a global company (with the help of ever so many capable and committed colleagues of many nationalities), I take even greater pride in having played a part in creating a well-defined culture that continues to define and differentiate the enterprise that bears my name.

Chapter 8

Public Service: Good Citizenship is Good Business

When I returned to New York from Army service in Europe in 1946, most of the people I knew, other than the two clients that enabled me to start my own business, were business magazine editors and reporters I had cultivated when I was doing publicity for the big engineer-builder I worked for. Immediately, I resumed my earlier practice of lunch dates with reporters/editors several times a week, even when I did not have a specific story I wanted to place. My assumption, in addition to having a friend when I needed a placement, was that, from time to time, they would be asked to recommend a public relations consultant and I wanted my name to be "top of mind" with them. Actually, it worked. In 1948, Hartley W. Barclay, a business writer at *The New York Times*, recommended me to the American Watch Assemblers Association and I got the account. And it was through another friend at *The New York Times*, Harry Leather, that I met Bill Marsteller in 1952.

In my previous pre-army job, I was a one-person publicity department in addition to my assignment as aide to the CEO. I was responsible mainly for travel arrangements, his appointment schedule and reminding him of his promises and commitments. I knew only a handful of publicists and the term "public relations" was just entering my vocabulary. I was determined to know others in my line of business and was fortunate in meeting one of the most respected (and, for me, most memorable) public relations counselors of the time, one G. Edward Pendray. Pendray's then mid-sized firm (about a dozen people) represented Brookhaven National Laboratory where my client, Ferguson, was designing and building the first nuclear reactor for the peaceful use of atomic energy. Before starting his business, Pendray was senior public relations officer at Westinghouse, in those days an industrial giant. He was well-known for creating the Westinghouse "time capsule" at the 1939 New York World's Fair. The capsule contained artifacts of the pre-World War II era and was buried at a site on the fairgrounds. It would be opened a century later. He also was a cohort of rocket pioneer Charles Goddard and was actively promoting the space age in the 1930s. In 1948, Pendray proposed me for membership in the National Association of Public Relations Counsel, which a few years later joined with another group to form today's Public Relations Society of America (PRSA).

At that time, PRSA was the gathering place for the country's top public relations executives. Regular attendants at its meeting were powerful people like John Hill (Hill & Knowlton), George Hammond (Carl Byoir & Associates), Tommy Ross (Ivy Lee and T. J. Ross), Pendleton Dudley (Dudley Anderson & Yutzy), Farley Manning and Jim Selvage (Manning Selvage & Lee), Kal Druck (Harshe Rotman & Druck) and on the corporate side, Kerryn King (Texaco), Harold Brayman (DuPont), Tony DeLorenzo (General Motors), Bob Fegley (General Electric), Lee Jaffe (New York Port Authority). I started working on PRSA committees and soon got to know most of the mighty in public relations – among them the one-of-a-kind Denny Griswold who edited *Public Relations News* for almost fifty years, the self-appointed doyenne and guardian of public relations. For about ten years starting in the early 1960s the "in" party at PRSA annual conferences was hosted by Burson-Marsteller for 75/100 clients and prospects. We went all out selecting unique venues – an antebellum home in the French quarter in New Orleans, the Dodge mansion on the outskirts of Detroit, an 1890s home of a wealthy brewer in St. Louis, Villa Viscaya in Miami, San Diego's fabled zoo. We continued the parties until senior executives stopped attending PRSA conferences.

As noted earlier, I also was active in several other public relations organizations that brought me together with fellow entrepreneurs and practitioners both agency and corporate. Throughout my career I have learned from them and enjoyed their company and many became both clients and friends.

In the early 1970s – a time when the name Burson-Marsteller began to be recognized in the broader business community – I sought out opportunities in the not-for-profit sector to gain visibility. It was – and continues to be – my belief that public service is both good citizenship and good business. It's worked that way for me.

The public institution with which I have been most closely identified is the John F. Kennedy Center for the Performing Arts in Washington. My introduction to Kennedy Center dates back to 1973, only two years after it opened as a memorial to the assassinated president. It came about when Marsteller Advertising executive Dick Brecker told Jillian Poole, Kennedy Center's enterprising development director, that I might be helpful to her. Unbeknownst to Jillian, my cousin, Abe Fortas, a former U.S. Supreme Court Justice, was a Kennedy Center trustee and close confidante of its top executive Roger Stevens. On learning Jillian was interested in enlisting me as a resource, Abe encouraged me to participate and arranged for my election to the board of Kennedy Center Productions Inc., a private-citizen group that funded Kennedy Center initiatives, usually new plays. The play I remember most clearly started with a telephone call from Fortas. He was calling for Roger Stevens who wanted my vote to invest $250,000 to bring a new musical called "Annie" to Kennedy Center for which we would get a twenty-four percent interest. I told Abe that all I knew about "Annie" was "it got bad reviews at its New Haven preview." He responded that the play had been rewritten and "Roger thinks it will be a big hit." Since in addition to heading Kennedy Center, Stevens was one of Broadway's most successful producers, I felt I had little choice but to vote with him for making the investment. Kennedy Center's "take" from "Annie" exceeded $10 million.

Almost overnight, I became a Kennedy Center "insider" – but at the price of knowing I was there only because I was perceived to be someone who could help the Kennedy Center raise money from the corporate community. Happily, I can point to three situations I initiated which produced the favorable financial returns that were expected of me.

At a Kennedy Center Productions meeting in late 1974, an agenda item was "capitalizing on the U.S. Bicentennial to build the Center's unfinished fourth theater." Countries, industry groups and corporations at the time were planning

Bicentennial gifts and other undertakings to commemorate the two hundredth anniversary of the signing of the Declaration of Independence. Not fully realizing what was happening to me, Abe Fortas saddled me with responsibility for "raising three million dollars from your well-heeled corporate friends." He delighted in setting impossible goals that challenged one to prove his/her worth. I pleaded that I had no experience raising that much money and I was not even aware that a fourth theater was ever planned for Kennedy Center. I was quickly escorted to a vast "empty space" between the ceiling of the Eisenhower Theater and the underside of Kennedy Center roof. I later learned the small, intimate theater that was to have occupied that space was eliminated because the construction money ran out. Stevens and Fortas were determined to build the theater. Abe's interest was his love for chamber music and Kennedy Center had no suitable venue. Roger simply wanted to complete the originally planned structure. Both seemed certain I would unearth the benefactor(s) who would provide the wherewithal – $3 million in hard cash.

I decided early on it would be easier to get $3 million from a single donor than from multiple donors. But that was before I learned the gift did not provide a "naming" opportunity. The only names that can be associated with the cultural center on the Potomac, by act of Congress, are Kennedy and Eisenhower. Three serious prospective donors emerged, two corporations and one trade association representing a basic industry. Each of the three, I believed, had good reason to demonstrate in a dramatic manner their gratitude to their country on the occasion of its two hundredth birthday. But each of them respectfully declined, acknowledging the value of the cause but pleading bad timing from their individual perspectives.

While preparing for a business trip to our then-new office in Tokyo, it occurred to me that the Japanese business community and/or government ought to be interested in making a highly visible U.S. Bicentennial gift. After all, Americans were buying a lot of Toyotas, Datsuns (later Nissans), Sony and Panasonic electronic products and the Japanese economy was booming. The chairman of the Fuji Bank was, in a sense, my business partner and we were on the way to becoming friends. He also was a leader of the Keidanren, the Japanese equivalent of our Business Roundtable. I wrote him that I wished to make him aware of an opportunity that would be extremely beneficial to the Japanese business community when I visited Tokyo. He obliged by having CEOs of two other large corporations at our meeting, each of them a senior Keidanren officer.

The day we met was my fifty-fourth birthday, February 15, 1975. My first iteration to them of the proposal, calling for a gift of $3 million to build a four hundred-seat theater at Kennedy Center, was disappointingly underwhelming. They gave me a polite hearing, but I quickly realized that I had generated no enthusiasm for my cause. I then asked the direct question, "has the Japanese government and/or business community decided what its Bicentennial gift to the United States will be." After about two minutes of inside discussion (which, of course, I did not understand), I was told that the decision was not yet final, but it was likely that a Japanese rock garden would be created at the Freer Gallery of Art, a part of the Smithsonian complex. Later, I learned the Japanese government gift of cherry trees to Washington D.C. in the 1920s, a major success, inspired the choice of a rock garden.

Probably out of politeness, my hosts asked my opinion on the appropriateness of a rock garden as a Bicentennial gift. Having read books and articles on Japanese cultural sensitivity, I praised my hosts' generosity and their ingenuity. Then I posed the seemingly innocuous question, "are you also endowing the rock garden for perpetual care?" I soon learned that "perpetual care" is not a top of mind concept in Japan. Only when I explained that burial site purchases were often accompanied by arrangements for "perpetual care" did my friends grasp what I was asking them. I suggested that, though possessed of many virtues, one should not assume the U.S. Park Service has special expertise caring for Japanese rock gardens. Demonstrating some humility, my hosts then asked me to repeat my presentation on the theater at Kennedy Center. The session ended with the comment, "Mr. Burson, we thank you for saving us from a possible embarrassment." I was also told that my written proposal (translated into Japanese) would be discussed at the Keidanren and with appropriate Japanese government officials since such a gift had to be endorsed by Japan's legislative body, the Diet.

Reporting to Messrs. Stevens and Fortas, I evinced a modicum of optimism that Japan would come through for us. At the least, I was almost certain that Japan's Bicentennial gift to the United States gift would not be a rock garden. After my return to New York, an international bribery scandal dominated the Japanese Diet agenda for several months and the silence in Tokyo caused my friends at Kennedy Center to question my original optimism. Every other week, I telephoned friends in Japan to determine the status of the gift. Invariably, I was reassured that "the matter is where it should be at this time, considering the preoccupation of the Diet with other issues." As spring went into summer, it was delicately suggested that I should consider alternative donors.

Instead, I visited Burson-Marsteller offices in Europe during the month of July (one of my waggish associates once termed such visits as "Harold's definition of a vacation"). Returning from dinner in London late one evening, the telephone rang. It was Roger Stevens asking "do you know why the Japanese ambassador wants to see me in his office tomorrow morning?" I suggested to Roger that it was not likely that the Japanese ambassador would invite him to his office to give him bad news. Swallowing his words as was Roger's wont, he agreed. I then asked if Kennedy Center had any other matters pending with Japan. The answer was negative. I told Roger I suspected we had the money, but I would call Tokyo for confirmation. My call to my Japanese friend was greeted with, "I tried to reach you in New York. The Diet approved the gift of three million dollars this afternoon."

A few months later, Prime Minister Miti made a state visit to Washington. He brought with him a check for $3 million. President Ford received it in the Rose Garden on behalf of Kennedy Center. My wife Bette and I were invited to the state luncheon honoring the Prime Minister. I was one of four trustees responsible for selecting the renowned architect Philip Johnson to design The Terrace Theater. The opening event in 1979 was a Kabuki performance paid for by the Japanese government. Although President Carter was scheduled to attend, a conflict developed and I escorted First Lady Roslyn Carter and Amy to the opening. Since that time, The Terrace Theater has provided a venue for all manner of chamber music and solo offerings and even mini-opera. It is a jewel of a theater – once a "big hole in the ceiling" above the Eisenhower Theater.

⎯⎯ ∞ ⎯⎯

The idea for a "national center for the performing arts" arose during the Eisenhower administration when a tract of property in Foggy Bottom along the Potomac was put up for sale by Washington's gas company. Congress appropriated funds to buy the land but not enough to construct a theater complex. Congress continued to refuse construction funds for the better part of a decade despite public fervor for a cultural center worthy of our nation's capital. Two months after President Kennedy was assassinated in November 1963, Congress passed legislation establishing The John F. Kennedy Center for the Performing Arts as a memorial to the slain President and provided $23 million subject to raising a like amount from the private sector. When that condition was met, Congress authorized a loan from the U.S. Treasury for an additional $20 million to be repaid after ten years. It was an odd financing arrangement for a presidential memorial whose total cost was about $70 million dollars.

The corporate sector contributed a substantial fraction of the private sector funds. But after the three theaters were built – the Opera House, the Eisenhower Theater and the Concert Hall – no sustained effort was made to enlist business support on a continuing basis. Instead, when funds were required for musical or theatrical productions whose cost exceeded ticket sales, Kennedy Center's development office contacted corporations for grants to cover the deficit. In return, the donor was named as a sponsor in programs and promotional materials. When Jillian Poole described this process to me, I thought it was a scary way to live – calling on corporations, hat in hand, at the last minute for funding for a scheduled production. Instead, I proposed a mechanism that would provide continuing corporate support. The result was The Kennedy Center Corporate Fund.

The case for corporate support for Kennedy Center is easy to make, although we would soon learn that many companies whose headquarters are distant from the nation's capital argued "we support our local symphony and ballet company in Houston or Cincinnati or Minneapolis so why should we support a performing arts center in Washington?" Our response was simply that Washington is our country's most visited tourist destination and the primary international gathering place for government officials and leaders in all walks of life. Families, friends, employees, customers and business associates of all major U.S. corporations regularly visit Washington and, until the arrival of Kennedy Center, were deprived of a world class cultural experience. It was an easy argument to make.

My idea was to name a board of governors of approximately twenty chief executives of leading corporations who would contribute themselves and seek donations from their business counterparts. We arranged for the announcement of the Kennedy Center Corporate Fund to be made by President Gerald Ford at The White House in November 1976, a strategy that positioned the fund as a national philanthropic priority. And we were fortunate in enlisting Don McNaughton, CEO, Prudential Insurance, to be its first chairman. The fact that McNaughton was chairman of the prestigious Business Roundtable was a major factor in attracting participation and financial support from his peer group. Among CEOs who followed McNaughton as chairman of the Kennedy Center Corporate Fund are Jack Welch, General Electric; James E. Burke and Ralph Larsen, Johnson & Johnson; John DeButts and Charles Brown, AT&T; Rawleigh Warner, Mobil; Roger Smith, General Motors; Frank Carey, IBM; and Ed Woollard, DuPont. The first year we raised a million-and-a-half dollars and in the past quarter century we have raised a total of almost $100 million.

Mine is the only name listed as a "governor" throughout the entire history of the fund. Because of this association, I have met literally scores of CEOs of *FORTUNE* 500 companies over the past quarter century.

∞∞∞

Abe Fortas died in April 1982. Bette and I were in Tokyo and had returned to our hotel about midnight. When traveling abroad in those pre-CNN days, I relied on Armed Forces Radio Service for the news. The lead item on the newscast was that Abe Fortas was dead at age 72, the result of a ruptured aortic artery. Since he had never mentioned having a heart problem and was vigorously healthy when I had seen him less than a fortnight earlier, I was both surprised and saddened. We had had a relatively close relationship from the time I first visited him in Washington in 1941. He was then 31 years old and was undersecretary of the Interior. I recall even today that his office was the size of a tennis court.

In the last two decades of his life, Fortas played a leading role making Kennedy Center a national center for the performing arts. One of President Johnson's most trusted political advisers and personal friends, he had considerable influence on cultural matters at the White House. I felt his extraordinary contribution to Kennedy Center should be memorialized in a lasting manner.

Starting in high school Fortas had a deep-seated passion for music. He was a highly competent classical violinist whose talents were recognized by world class musicians. Isaac Stern was among his closest friends and the two often played recreational duets or participated in living room string quartets. Intuitively, I thought it made sense to marry Abe's passion for chamber music with his abiding interest in The Terrace Theater. After he had goaded me into finding a patron who would finance its construction, he and I were among the four trustees who had oversight for its design and construction. In fact, Roger Stevens often referred to The Terrace Theater as "Abe's chamber music playpen."

Stevens favored my idea of memorializing Fortas with a trust fund that would endow a continuing series of chamber music concerts at The Terrace Theater.

Carolyn Agger Fortas, Abe's widow was also supportive and even suggested names of friends and clients who would be likely contributors. Most important, Carol directed me to Bella Linden, a New York attorney with whom Abe collaborated through the years whose specialty was representing classical music artists and institutions.

Our goal was modest – we wanted to create an endowment to underwrite two chamber music series a year. We were advised that a million dollars would be adequate. The first two solicitations that Bella Linden and I made resulted in one-quarter of our goal. The late John Loeb Sr., an eminent investment banker, donated $125,000, followed by a gift in the same amount by the late Arnold Bernhard, founder of the Value Line investment group. Loeb had been a long-time Fortas friend and client. Bernhard's relationship was of more recent vintage as client and neighbor in Westport, Conn., where Carol and Abe had a summer home for many years. Several additional gifts came in at the $100,000 level (most of the major donors had not previously contributed to Kennedy Center). Though we fell a bit short of the million dollar goal, we had sufficient funds to launch the Fortas Chamber Music Concerts in the 1983-84 season.

While Carol Agger Fortas was interested in our money-raising efforts, neither Bella nor I asked her to contribute, nor did she offer. For a decade after Abe's death, Carol joined my wife, Bette, and me at the Kennedy Center Honors gala on the first Sunday in December. For the first few years, she was my guest, but when the price of admission increased, she insisted on paying for her ticket and Kennedy Center always accommodated us with three seats together in a front orchestra row. As soon as the final applause ended, my task was to rush to the bar for a generously-poured double Jack Daniels on the rocks for Carol. She sipped it slowly while smoking her post-performance cigar, and, on more than one occasion, asked for a refill.

Kennedy Center Honors night was an annual ritual for the three of us until Carol became afflicted with Alzheimer's disease in the early nineties. In what was to be our last conversation, she inquired about the Fortas chamber music concerts. I reported it was ongoing as planned, although I bemoaned the fact that the passing years had seen the loss of many of the classical music audience who still recognized the Fortas name. Her rather indeterminate response was something to the effect, "it would be a shame not to continue the series in view of Abe's great personal and professional commitment to Kennedy Center and his passion for chamber music." Following her death five years later, she bequeathed one-third of her approximately $25 million estate to the Abe Fortas Memorial Fund, (Barnard College and the Yale Law School received equal amounts). Today the fund has more than $10 million in assets. That will buy a lot of chamber music! I continue to be one of the fund's trustees.

My association with Kennedy Center led to another Washington undertaking that I found stimulating and, I believe, served the public interest. For as long as Roger Stevens headed Kennedy Center, he tried unsuccessfully to get me a presidential appointment to the Kennedy Center Board of Trustees. Once, however, I came close. In the waning days of the Carter administration, I received word that my name was on the list of new appointees – recognition for my services to Kennedy Center over the past decade (I had no "special" connection to the Carter White House, although I know Press Secretary Jody Powell). During the last week of the Carter presidency, Terry Straub, an assistant to President Carter who later joined U.S. Steel and whom I came to know and respect, telephoned me the bad news that my name was dropped as a Kennedy Center appointee in favor of a relative of a Carter political adviser. Having read my supporting data, Terry thought I was getting a raw deal and, as a consolation, told me I could have one of two appointments still available before President Carter left office. One was as a member of the oversight board of the federal prison system. The other was as a member of the Commission of Fine Arts. It didn't take long for me to decide I wanted no part of the federal prison system. But I asked Terry if he would keep the Fine Arts Commission offer open for just a few hours – until I could talk with J. Carter Brown, the Commission's long-time chairman whom I had met through Kennedy Center. My question to Carter Brown was simply, "do you think I can make a contribution as a member of the commission." He said he would welcome my appointment and that it was "in keeping with the legislation establishing the Commission" that called for "representatives of the public interest" in addition to architects, artists, sculptors and others in the fine arts community. I telephoned my acceptance to Terry Straub and thanked him for his efforts in my behalf. My appointment to the Commission of Fine Arts, signed by Jimmy Carter, is dated January 18, 1981, just forty-eight hours before Ronald Reagan was inaugurated as the fortieth President of the United States.

The Commission of Fine Arts is a super zoning board for three specific areas in the District of Columbia: the Federal Triangle, Georgetown and areas contiguous to Rock Creek Park. When I joined, the members included two distinguished architects, an eminent landscape architect, a Washington real estate developer, a Carter supporter in Pennsylvania and its chairman, the then director of the National Gallery of Art and one of the most personable and resourceful individuals I have ever known and worked with. The two projects that interested me most during my five years on the Commission were the ongoing Pennsylvania Avenue Redevelopment and the Vietnam War Memorial.

The Pennsylvania Avenue project called for reviewing and approving architectural design for a dozen or so major buildings on the majestic corridor that connects the Capitol with the area immediately adjacent to The White House. They included the Canadian Embassy, the JW Marriott Hotel and the office building extension of the Willard Hotel. We were even able to preserve the traditional period facades on Pennsylvania Avenue fronting the new George Washington University building several blocks west of The White House. The Commission was unanimous in wanting to retain the institutional quality of the extra-width boulevard traversed every four years by newly sworn-in Presidents to their home a mile or so distant on Pennsylvania Avenue. Almost without exception, the Commission deferred approval of architectural plans on the first submission. Usually, revisions involved changes in colors or textures of building materials (usually more subdued), further setbacks of upper floors to retain a consistent height line when viewed from street level or, in one instance, to reduce building mass to conform to other structures along the avenue. One evening, I remember Commission members gathering at nightfall along Pennsylvania Avenue in mid-winter to determine which of several lighting standards would line both sides of the avenue and to decide a specific illumination intensity. Nowadays, when I travel Pennsylvania Avenue between the Treasury Building and Capitol Hill, I take pride in having been one of seven whose taste and judgment are reflected in the architectural legacy that we had a role in fashioning.

Perhaps the most exciting and suspenseful building project in the near hundred year history of the Commission of Fine Arts was the Vietnam Memorial. Few would disagree that the war itself was one of the most divisive events since the Civil War. The intense division grew from the time a design submitted by a twenty-one year old Yale architecture student, Maya Lin, was selected in a competition against hundreds of other entries. Her design was a wide-angled V-shaped black granite wall exceeding five hundred feet in length on which were engraved the names of the more than fifty thousand American soldiers who lost their lives in Vietnam in the order in which they died. The monument was located on the National Mall on a plot paralleling Constitution Avenue about a hundred yards east of the Lincoln Memorial, one of Washington's most-visited historical sites. Opposition to the design formed even before the design was formally presented for approval by the Fine Arts Commission. The principal objection to Maya Lin's design was that it was said to be "a tombstone" that failed to recognize the heroism of the men and women who gave their lives in the cause of freedom – "a black gash in the earth" was one description. The opposition was led by former Vietnam veterans who had support from one member of Congress in particular and, subsequently, from Ross Perot, who, at the time, was believed to have presidential aspirations.

Anticipating opposition at the open Commission meeting at which the Vietnam Memorial design was to be presented, Carter Brown asked me to meet with him beforehand. He had reviewed Maya Lin's plans as soon as they were formally submitted to the Commission and was enthralled with the design. But he believed, and I concurred, that those antagonistic to her design would aggressively challenge it. Commission of Fine Arts approval was only one of several required for a memorial on the National Mall. Others had to come from the Secretary of the Interior who has oversight of federal land; the National Park Service, which maintains and manages national monuments, and other planning groups. At the Commission meeting, we expected a protest demonstration by Vietnam veterans that would make the evening television news. In the face of all that angst, Carter Brown was determined to preserve the integrity of the Maya Lin design and he skillfully presented his case to each of the Commission members. Perhaps fortuitously, the Commission was unanimous in its support of the original design from the outset.

The law governing the Commission of Fine Arts provides a formal challenge procedure and proponents of "a more heroic monument" called for a second hearing on the Maya Lin design. In addition to their general dislike of what they believed was a massive gravestone, they bemoaned the lack of an American flag and the absence of soldiers. On the basis of their public statements, they appeared to want both the flag and some representation of soldiers in battle mode to be inserted at the apex of the "V" which, of course, would have seriously compromised the original design. To assure continued solidarity among the seven members of the Commission at a time when one or two members may have been amenable to what Chairman Brown considered an inappropriate accommodation to the group that considered themselves the "true patriots," Brown called for a recess of the second meeting to get a firsthand view of the monument site. He had arranged for the rental of a large van that accommodated the full Commission and, on the drive from the Commission's headquarters to the site near the Lincoln Memorial, he revealed the details of a compromise which he felt would protect the integrity and spirit of the original design and hopefully mollify those opposed to the original design. One element called for erecting a flagpole about a hundred feet to the west of the granite wall's terminus where a large American flag that could be seen by those visiting both the Vietnam Memorial and the Lincoln Memorial. The other element called for a sculpture of four figures in military dress to be placed in a wooded area a hundred or more yards distant from the wall. The sculpture would consist of three males – a Caucasian, an African-American and a Hispanic – in a posture that approximated patrol duty and one female, a nurse. The mood of the Commission was to stand firm, but Brown patiently outlined the "politics" that could defer construction indefinitely. Maya Lin was highly protective of her original design; she let it be known that she felt that any accommodation would compromise her design. After further open discussion, Carter Brown's compromise was accepted and Maya Lin's design became what today is one of Washington's most visited monuments.

Although I very likely could have remained a member of the Commission after my term expired, I chose to retire. I had been a party to preserving the majesty of Pennsylvania Avenue and to memorializing in a tasteful manner the 50,000-plus Americans who lost their lives in Vietnam. Also, I had been a member of the Commission for one of only two occasions when it was overruled. The first was when President Truman added a small balcony to the second floor on the South side of The White House. The Commission of which I was a member was overruled by the Mayor of Washington when we denied approval for building a large commercial/residential structure on the Potomac in Georgetown because its large scale would create traffic problems.

It was only natural for me to be interested in the U.S. Information Agency from the time it was formed during the Eisenhower Administration. My first active involvement was in the early 1960s after President Kennedy appointed the premier television anchorman of the day, Edward R. Murrow of CBS, to be its director. Murrow appointed a private sector advisory committee and I was one of its members. While I continued to maintain contact with USIA directors in subsequent administrations, I did not seriously reengage myself until Charles Wick was appointed by President Reagan to head the agency. Wick expanded private sector involvement exponentially. Among others, he created a private sector public relations advisory committee chaired by my friend Henry Rogers, the co-founder of the Rogers & Cowan public relations firm. Henry asked me to join. In the process, Charles became one of my close friends (and he and his wife, Mary Jane, remained so some two decades later). At the end of President Reagan's first term, Henry stepped down as chairman and I succeeded him.

The USIA Private Sector Public Relations Advisery Committee consisted of approximately twenty of the country's leading public relations executives from both corporations and public relations firms, in the main organizations with global reach. Our role was totally advisery, although from time to time various members served both as a resource to USIA public affairs officers in embassies around the world as well as linkages to the private sector. We met quarterly and, almost invariably, had perfect attendance for the briefings we received from Director Wick, Richard Carlson, who headed the Voice of America, and other senior USIA executives. Our members were frequently asked to provide input and critique for USIA policy and communications initiatives. When Charles Wick retired after eight years as the longest serving director of USIA, I hosted his retirement party at the Pan-American Union. The special guest of the evening was President Reagan and I exercised my prerogative as host by seating myself next to him. (Wick was his other seat mate and the table included Katharine Graham, publisher of *The Washington Post,* seated next to me and Roberto Goizueta, CEO of our client, The Coca-Cola Company.) Although I had had receiving line encounters with other presidents and was once briefly with President Reagan in the Oval Office, this was the first time I had ever had two hours' face time with a President of the United States. Some months later, after he left the presidency, I was to become more closely associated with President Reagan, but that evening in November 1988 when I hosted 347 guests, one of them the President of the United States, was one I will never forget. Yes, I was sad that my mother had not lived to see it!

Chapter 9

❧

The Thrill of Landing a New Client:
Two Cases, General Motors and Coca-Cola

Anyone who has ever worked at a public relations firm (or an advertising agency) knows what a thrill it is to land a new client. Even at my stage of the game, I get charged up knowing that one or another Burson-Marsteller office has bagged a big one.

"New business" had a high priority at Burson-Marsteller from the outset. Our first year revenues were about a hundred thousand dollars. While we expected growth from our few existing clients, our success depended on attracting new clients. As discussed earlier, we were fortunate in having a ready-made list of prospects, the Marsteller Advertising roster of clients. But from the start, I measured success against the biggest and best independent public relations firms and that meant winning clients totally on our own merit.

Gaining new clients is important even for a business as mature as today's Burson-Marsteller. There's nothing that more quickly boosts morale, unites a company, which is spread across five continents, and universally evokes pride and a sense of belonging. New business is the most visible sign of progress, a payoff for good performance for existing clients, and a manifestation of success to existing clients, prospective clients and the public relations community overall.

Growth also provides the wherewithal for increased compensation and creates opportunities for promotions into jobs of greater responsibility.

After we built a nucleus of clients that gave us reason to believe we had a stable business – a decade long process until we reached a million dollars in annual revenues – our objective was to achieve annual revenue growth of not less than fifteen percent. If we made it, we would double in size every five years. We wanted half of our growth to come from existing clients – doing that would prove ongoing clients valued our services. The remaining half had to come from new clients – that would prove we were measuring up to our competition.

At that time, each of our offices was headed by a general manager whose primary responsibility was managing his/her part of the business by growing revenues and profits. In addition to making myself available for locally-generated new business solicitations and presentations (I hate the word "pitch" – whether it's "pitching" a client or "pitching" a story), I had my own "wish list," companies I wanted on the Burson-Marsteller client list and I made it my business to get us a time at bat.

Two of the companies on my wish list were General Motors and Coca-Cola.

In 1957, we made a joint presentation with Marsteller Advertising for GM's non-auto Electro-Motive Division, the world's leading manufacturer of locomotives, headquartered at La Grange, Ill. We jointly got the business and that enabled me and Buck Buchwald to establish a working relationship with Anthony G. (Tony) DeLorenzo, the widely-respected vice president in charge of the General Motors public relations staff, then about 300 people. Despite my hope that one day we might work for General Motors either at the corporate level or for one of the car divisions, I considered the prospects bleak because of the large internal staff – whose competence Buck and I quickly learned to appreciate from our Electro-Motive vantage point.

Coca-Cola, during a good part of the 1970s, employed Ruder·Finn as its public relations firm. Previously, Coca-Cola worked with the Steve Hannegan firm (whose reputation was based largely on successfully promoting Miami Beach and Sun Valley as resort destinations) and Thomas J. Deegan, a well-positioned boutique in New York and Washington (Tom Deegan, who became a friend, headed the New York World's Fair Corporation in the 1960s). For many years, Coca-Cola headed my "wish list" — undoubtedly a factor of my early years in Memphis and the south. But I respected the Ruder·Finn association and felt it would be a long time before I could aggressively go after Coca-Cola.

Here, then, is the story of how these two great corporations became Burson-Marsteller clients.

———⬡⬡⬡———

In 1970, General Motors was the principal, highly visible target of the then-young consumer activist Ralph Nader in his aggressive attack on the U.S. auto industry. The issue he exploited was safety. His book, *Unsafe at Any Speed*, aimed specifically at GM design practices, was an immediate best-seller. Soon Nader was testifying before Congressional committees as were the Big Three auto CEOs. General Motors, then the world's largest corporation, bore the brunt of the media attacks, both print and electronic. One Congressional hearing produced such a public outcry that GM's board of directors created a Committee on Public Policy and Social Responsibility that specifically directed management to employ outside public relations counsel.

Our involvement started with a surprise telephone call in late June 1970 from Tony DeLorenzo, vice president, public relations staff, to tell me Burson-Marsteller was one of three firms selected as contenders to be public relations counsel for General Motors. The others were, predictably, Hill & Knowlton and Carl Byoir & Associates, then the two largest and most highly regarded firms in the field. It was made clear from the outset that GM management was interested in obtaining public relations counsel at the corporation's most senior level. They had no interest in hiring "arms and legs" to implement programs or projects – they did that internally.

The first step, we were told, would be a meeting with DeLorenzo and Oscar Lundeen, GM vice chairman and the board member charged with overseeing the search for a public relations firm. Buck Buchwald and I had spent the preceding two weeks researching automobile issues and, in particular, how the media treated General Motors (before the Internet that was a formidable task!). We believed our only chance of winning the business would be by demonstrating, first, that we knew more about the auto industry and its issues than our competitors, and, second, by being brutally candid with our prospective client. Buck and I agreed to "tell it like it is" even though what we said would likely not be what GM executives wanted to hear – or what they had been hearing from internal advisers. At the time, this was a bold approach. General Motors was the world's most successful corporation measured by almost any metric, and an aura of infallibility permeated its management structure. Outsiders, especially consultants, played an insignificant role in the then closed General Motors culture.

That first meeting with Lundeen and DeLorenzo took place at GM's elegantly furnished offices on the twenty-fifth floor of the then newly-erected General Motors Building facing the Plaza Hotel on Fifth Avenue. Buck and I took turns telling them that General Motors was widely perceived to be arrogant, fearsomely powerful and studiedly unresponsive to its numerous publics, including the government, franchised dealers and even customers. As we walked back to our office at 866 Third Avenue, neither Buck nor I was certain we would be called back for a second meeting – this time with GM's austere CEO James Roche (who turned out to be a kind and considerate client). The next day DeLorenzo telephoned me with the comment "you guys were pretty rough on us, but you got Oscar Lundeen's attention." He said he would call me "in a week or so" but stopped short of saying we would go to the second step and meet with Jim Roche. Nor did he say or infer we had talked ourselves out of the business.

A few nail-biting days later, the call came to schedule a meeting with Messrs. Roche and Lundeen in the executive suite of GM headquarters in Detroit. Buck and I agonized over the approach we should take in the second and what we were told would be the final round in the competition. We decided to stay on course with our bare bones version of how we felt General Motors was perceived and the need for attitudinal and behavioral changes in how they related to their numerous constituencies. It had worked with Lundeen, GM's No. 2 executive; we could only hope it would work with Roche, GM's No. 1 executive.

That second meeting went well. Roche defended the GM record, admitted to a degree of insulation from some GM stakeholders as well as a need to be more proactive in gaining a greater understanding of General Motors. The essence of his message, as I recall it, was "General Motors is a great and public-spirited company, but we have ignored the importance of public perceptions in the framing and implementation of our policies and we must do something to change that." We were told that "it may be a while – a month or so" before a decision on which of the three agencies they would work with. They explained that GM management was immersed in the auto industry's upcoming labor negotiations. Buck and I were, of course, aware of media speculation that both the industry and the union would take hard-line positions and that a strike was likely. General Motors was believed to be the United Auto Workers' probable target.

Not hearing from DeLorenzo for three weeks, I telephoned him in Detroit. He explained in a friendly way that the reason "you have not heard anything" was, simply, that he and other GM senior executives were "tied up with the labor negotiations." He said the public relations issue would not get senior management attention until a settlement was reached, certainly not before October. As speculated, GM was the target company and there was a strike – six long weeks during which DeLorenzo and I exchanged telephone calls and even visited over lunch when DeLorenzo was in New York. He played it close to the vest, but he assured us that the chemistry between Burson/Buchwald and the two most senior GM executives was good.

In late November, I got another telephone call from DeLorenzo: "Oscar (Lundeen) will be in New York next Monday for the board meeting and he wants to know if you'll be in your office Tuesday morning so that he can come see where you live." I told him we would welcome Lundeen's visit. Instantly, I knew the game was over and we had won! I can't remember an occasion that gave me a greater thrill. Oscar Lundeen, the second most powerful executive at the world's largest and most profitable corporation, would hardly traipse around New York City examining the premises of three public relations firms. His visit to our office at 866 Third Avenue would be to deliver the good news.

And so it came to pass. Burson-Marsteller had received the equivalent of the corporate Good Housekeeping Seal of Approval.

Today's business leaders have little appreciation of General Motors's preeminent position in the corporate firmament for the four decades following World War II. GM was so much larger, so much more profitable and so far advanced over other corporations in its management practices that it occupied its own exclusive niche atop the pinnacle of the world business pyramid. For a year or more after winning the General Motors business, the questions most often asked me by client CEOs involved our relationship with General Motors. And I have long believed that adding General Motors to our client list was the "defining moment" that sparked the growth spurt that continued for more than two decades with double digit annual revenue increases and propelled us to the No. 1 position as the world's largest public relations firm in 1983.*

---------- ∞ ----------

Of the hundred or more corporate leaders I have worked with over the past half century, the most memorable was Roberto C. Goizueta, the gifted and charismatic chairman and chief executive officer of The Coca-Cola Company

General Motors was a Burson-Marsteller client for eleven years. Following our acquisition by Young & Rubicam, we took the initiative in ending the relationship in 1981. Tony DeLorenzo, who has a place in my personal pantheon of public relations "greats," had retired and we were just starting to work with our fourth GM CEO. We took the action to work with Y&R in pursuing Ford business.

from 1981 until 1997. In my view, he was one-of-a-kind on the American corporate scene. With the possible exception of John F. (Jack) Welch, CEO at General Electric, no one of his generation left so distinguished an imprint on a major corporation. When he died on October 16, 1997, less than two months after he learned he had lung cancer, leading business publications around the world not only noted his death with lead articles, but many followed up with editorials and reflective treatises on the special qualities he brought to Coca-Cola and the world of global business.

Roberto and I met in 1980 when he was one of six vice chairmen of Coca-Cola in the succession horse race to follow the ailing Paul Austin as Coke's CEO. Our meeting came about after two visits I had made to Atlanta trying to make Coca-Cola a Burson-Marsteller client.

In those days, new business was not much of a problem for Burson-Marsteller, especially in the U.S. Year-after-year, we grew at a rate of twenty percent or thereabouts. Mostly, it came from existing clients and from corporate executives who had heard about us and telephoned or wrote to say they wanted to hire us. And as I've said, Coca-Cola was on my personal "wish list" of corporations I really wanted on the Burson-Marsteller client list.

My first new business contact with Coca-Cola was in the late 1970s when an Ole Miss classmate, Lucian (Luke) Smith, was named president. Luke and I knew one another throughout the four years we were in Oxford (Mississippi, I should make clear!). His appointment happened to coincide with a change in Coca-Cola's relationship with its public relations firm, Ruder·Finn. That came about when R·F's largest client, Philip Morris, acquired 7-Up. Coca-Cola perceived this to be a conflict and Ruder·Finn had to choose between the two clients. They chose Philip Morris, thereby opening the door for a new public relations firm at Coca-Cola.

While Smith greeted me warmly, he explained that he had no voice in the selection of a public relations firm. He introduced me to William (Bill) Prewitt, Coke's director of public relations, then a relatively low level position in the company. Prewitt did not have the authority to hire a public relations firm. But, perhaps encouraged by my college friend, he paved the way for me to meet with those empowered to do so. Before leaving Atlanta, I met his boss, the late Garth Hamby, who informed me privately that a decision on selecting a public relations firm would be deferred for the time being. I subsequently learned that meant after a new chief executive officer was named.

Several months later, I visited Atlanta again for a second call on Garth Hamby.

He was one of the gentlest and most soft-spoken men I have met in business. At the same time, he exuded a persistence to get things done. We spoke for more than an hour about public relations in general and about some of the opportunities for Coca-Cola, a company that seemed to me to have lost its luster of earlier years. He admonished me to "keep in touch."

A month later, Garth telephoned me. He and his boss, whom he identified as Roberto Goizueta, would be in New York the following week. I invited the two of them to lunch in our company dining room on the nineteenth floor of 866 Third Avenue. That venue, I felt, would be quieter and more private than a restaurant or a club, and we employed a chef whose cuisine was widely praised by our guests.

The research I did on Goizueta did little to explain why he, as one of the six vice chairmen, was a contender for Coke's CEO position. Only recently had he been given overall responsibility for public and government affairs. He was a Cuban who emigrated to the United States in 1964. A Yale University graduate with a chemical engineering degree, he had joined Coca-Cola in Havana in 1954, his first job. Until he was appointed a vice chairman, his responsibilities at Coca-Cola had been engineering or technical in nature. I had not yet ascertained that, through the years, he had developed a close relationship with the late Robert Woodruff, a giant among corporate leaders who made Coca-Cola a worldwide business institution. Since Garth had made clear that Roberto wanted to talk informally with me and that they did not want to see a "dog and pony" show, the lunch table was set for the three of us.

What was to have been a twelve to two luncheon became an extended discussion that lasted until a few minutes short of four o'clock. I had never met anyone like Roberto Goizueta. Speaking with a pronounced accent, he employed the English language with great precision. He was well versed in current affairs and what he said reflected a large vocabulary. It was obvious that he was well-read. It was obvious, too, that he was a conceptual thinker. While he enjoyed talking about people and events, he was equally at ease in discussing ideas. It was also obvious that he was passionately committed to The Coca-Cola Company and that he had a vision for the company much more expansive than the company's performance of the recent past. Coca-Cola, he believed, was falling short in achieving its potential. That potential included not only growth in sales, earnings and the price of its stock, but also building relationships with the millions of people who stopped to "enjoy a Coke" at some time in their day. And it included making tens of thousands of people around the world proud to be members of the Coca-Cola system that delivers a billion servings a day.

Four months after that first and only meeting with him, I read in *The Wall Street Journal* that Roberto C. Goizueta had been elected chairman and chief executive officer of The Coca-Cola Company. I responded by sending him a handwritten note wishing him well and expressing the hope that we could meet soon to continue our discussion.

Garth telephoned me three weeks later.

"Will you be available to meet with Mr. Goizueta at the end of the day next Tuesday at the Coca-Cola suite at the Regency Hotel on Park Avenue?," he asked. Of course, I would. I arrived a few minutes before five o'clock and Roberto was expecting me. I was to learn that promptness was a near fetish for him. When he made a date, you knew he would be there on time. He began by apologizing that he could not ask me to join him for dinner because of a previous commitment. However, he had "at least an hour or even a few minutes more" to talk about "an arrangement" that would make available to him my personal services. He quickly made me feel at ease – two friends resuming a conversation. He said he had made an assessment of his strengths and weaknesses vis-á-vis his new responsibility as chief executive officer at Coca-Cola and concluded that he had had little experience in relating to the media, to the investor community and to the public at large. In effect, he wanted not only an adviser but a mentor who would teach him the basics of establishing good relationships with the communities that he considered important to Coca-Cola and to his success as its CEO.

Like many of his counterparts in the corporate world, Goizueta was never fully trusting or comfortable with reporters and editors. Although he had some favorites like John Huey, now editorial director in charge of all *Time* Inc. publications, whom he met when John was Atlanta bureau chief for *The Wall Street Journal*, he was untrusting of how writers would report on him and The Coca-Cola Company. Perhaps his most frequent expressions of displeasure came during the hours of six and seven in the morning when he was chauffeured to his office while scanning *The New York Times*, *The Wall Street Journal* and *The Atlanta Journal-Constitution*. With many ties to the company, *The Journal-Constitution* frequently reported on matters that Goizueta considered premature or, in some instances, simply gossip or speculation. On those occasions, members of the Coca-Cola public relations staff – Carlton Curtis, Randal (Randy) Donaldson and others, who dealt directly with the media, could expect a call from his car. When he considered the reporting especially egregious, he called Garth Hamby. After Garth's retirement, the calls went to Earl Leonard, Coke's senior vice president responsible for public and government relations.

Goizueta suggested that the original agreement between The Coca-Cola Company and Burson-Marsteller be confined to a personal consulting relationship involving him and me. I was to report directly to him. We agreed that I would make one or two visits a month to Atlanta (more if called for), that he would provide access for me to Coke's senior management so that I could learn the basics of the soft drink business, and that we would speak frequently on the telephone. He also said he would send me copies of reports and correspondence that would expand my knowledge base on the issues affecting the company. He suggested I visit Atlanta as soon as possible to meet with Garth, his executive assistant and, in effect, gatekeeper, "to work out a compensation arrangement and to get introduced to our top executives." As I prepared to depart, he again made it clear that I would report directly to him, but that we may at a later date discuss a relationship between the totality of Burson-Marsteller and The Coca-Cola Company. Also, he reiterated that he was employing me because he believed I would tell him what he should hear rather than tailor my messages in anticipation of what I or others thought he wanted to hear. And he wanted an outside point of view as well as reports on how other CEOs approached common problems. This was the start of a twelve year relationship that I suspect was among the closest ever between the CEO of a major corporation and a public relations consultant.

Garth Hamby and I quickly agreed on a fixed monthly fee to cover my consulting services. Out-of-pocket for travel and other expenses would be reimbursed, and any projects requiring Burson-Marsteller staffers in addition to me would be billed separately at standard rates. The agreement also called for a review after three months to assess whether the fee was sufficient to fully compensate Burson-Marsteller for my services.

During the first two years when I worked as a personal consultant to Goizueta, Burson-Marsteller received several marketing assignments that produced minimal income at a time when our business was booming. My associates responsible for our business in New York were naturally eager to "grow the Coca-Cola business" and make it a meaningful Burson-Marsteller client from a revenue standpoint. I tried to assure them that their wish would come to pass but I did not think it prudent to force the issue. (In fact, I later learned that my relationship with Coca-Cola and Roberto Goizueta was sometimes referred to by my close associates as "Burson's ego trip.")

A little over two years into our relationship with Coca-Cola, Tom Mosser and Bill Noonan, two of my most senior associates at B-M/New York (sad to say, both have passed on) walked into my office and said "Barry Holt has offered us $30,000 a month to represent Pepsi International – twice as much as we billed Coke – what do you want to do?" They also told me Barry wanted "to get together with them within the next four or five days to talk." Barry had been a long-time and valued B-Mer who left in 1981 to join Pepsi and like so many others, continued to have an allegiance to Burson-Marsteller and its people. He had recently been promoted to head Pepsi International marketing communications and turned to his former colleagues for help. Although I valued my close relationship with Coca-Cola and with Roberto Goizueta and his management team – in particular, Don Keough, his second-in-command, I recognized that I was responsible for doing what was best overall (and long-term) for our business.

I telephoned Garth and told him it was important for me to have a face-to-face meeting with Roberto within the next 24/48 hours. He asked if I could tell him the reason for my wanting to see him so urgently. I told Garth what had transpired with my associates and that I wanted Roberto to know firsthand from me about it so that he could understand the position it put me in with my associates. Garth said he would call me back. Twenty minutes later we were on the phone again. "Come to Atlanta for lunch with the chairman and me tomorrow. But get here a half hour early so the two of us can talk before you meet Roberto."

At 11:30 the next morning I was in Garth Hamby's office. "After you have gone through your pleasantries when you meet in his private dining room, stop talking. Just let Roberto do the talking," he advised me. And that's what I did – just listened to my friend and client, Roberto Gouzieta. "Harold," he said, "I have been talking with Ike Herbert (Coke's top marketing officer) and we believe it's time that Burson-Marsteller played a bigger role with our company. I know it's hard to estimate how much work there will be, but you can count on about $35,000 a month – in addition to our personal arrangement –and we should start right away."

And so began the Burson-Marsteller relationship with Coca-Cola that continues to this day. (When I recently telephoned Barry Holt, now corporate vice president for global communications at Whirlpool, to verify some dates, I told him this story. "Now, at last I know why Tom and Bill cancelled that date we had," he commented.)

⊷∞⊶

Despite today's greater competitive environment, despite the RFP (Request for Proposal) process that has, in my view, diminished what we do as public relations professionals on both the agency and the client sides of the equation, despite the extravaganzas agencies feel forced to generate to demonstrate their creativity – knowing the telephone is ringing to tell you "the business is yours!" remains for me one of the greatest of all experiences in the agency business. And even more so when I was on the team that made it happen.

Chapter 10

❦

There's Nothing New Under the Sun: Most Likely,
Your "New" Idea is Really Old Hat

B y my reckoning, admittedly arbitrary, a generation in the world of public
relation nowadays spans about ten years, maybe less. Pre-1990, it was
longer – fifteen to twenty years. But with today's people turnover rate at
both public relations firms and corporate and not-for profit employers, there is
substantial replacement of staff every ten years.

Invariably, each new generation believes it is on the professional cutting edge
both strategically and tactically. And why not when the media covering public
relations, themselves subject to the same rate of generational change, so freely use
such descriptors in their reporting as "new," "the first" and, all too often, "revolutionary." But the fact is, if you've done something unique that works, chances
are that it's been done before. So my counsel would be to "go slow" when claim-
ing a "first" – or that you and your associates have come up with an idea that's
really new.

———❦———

Burson-Marsteller took on its first major public affairs assignments in the late 1960s. In quick succession, we were working on three highly visible issues covered by the national media, print and electronic. One involved the pesticide DDT, manufactured by our client, Stauffer Chemical. This was one of the very early environmental crises resulting from Rachel Carson's book, *Silent Spring*. The trigger was the discovery that the shells of peregrine falcon nesting eggs were becoming thin and fragile, a condition that threatened the species. Scientific investigation indicated that DDT residue on foliage ingested by peregrine falcons was to blame. While our client tried to salvage the product with what were then believed to be appropriate usage restrictions, it became apparent that DDT's future in the U.S. was doomed. In countries that had no peregrine falcons, many of them impoverished and suffering the ravages of mosquito-borne malaria, a case was made to continue spraying DDT over affected areas. In time, however, DDT was banned worldwide even though it was the most economical and effective weapon against malaria.

Another early environmental assignment was defending phosphates as a detergent ingredient. Phosphates is the substance that enables detergent marketers to claim "whiter than white" washing results. Without phosphates, white shirts would have a grayish look. Conventional wisdom among early environmentalists, however, was that phosphates, an organic material, was nourishing plant life growth in streams and rivers where detergent-containing effluent was disposed. This process is known as "eutrophication" and it was reducing the marine population because the surplus plant life consumed oxygen that had previously nurtured the fish. Lake Erie was frequently cited as an example. We argued on behalf of our client, FMC Corporation, the nation's largest supplier of phosphates, that phosphates were not the real culprit. A team in our Washington office defined the problem as a failure to treat sewage properly before its discharge into the nation's streams and lakes. We brought the issue to the attention of the League of Women Voters, and sewage treatment became an LWV priority. Reflecting consumer preference for "whiter than white" shirts and bed linen, efforts to ban phosphates at national and state levels were repelled and phosphates continued to be a detergent ingredient. The problem was resolved by constructing more efficient sewage disposal facilities that neutralized phosphates and other nutrients in the effluent.

A third early Burson-Marsteller public affairs assignment involved disposal of taconite tailings into Lake Superior in the late 1960s. It was our first application of what we now term "litigation support" (three or four decades earlier, the fabled publicist Ivy Lee performed a similar task for the Rockefeller family). Taconite, a natural ore found in Minnesota, is used to make steel. After the ore is taken from the ground, it is processed into small pebbles that are fed into steel furnaces. Left over from the pebble-forming process is an inert residue known as taconite "tailings." These tailings were disposed of by "dumping" them into Lake Superior. Reserve Mining Company, whose major owner was our client Armco Steel, was attacked by environmentalists and later sued by the federal government for polluting Lake Superior, a case that required years of litigation. Reserve Mining contended that taconite tailings dumped into the lake were totally inert, and the company produced scientific evidence that neither water quality nor marine life suffered any ill effects. The exacerbating problem was that about twenty square miles of the lake, the portion near shore where the taconite tailings were dumped, looked darker than the surrounding lake from the air (it did not reflect the sunlight in the way the natural bottom did). But we could not convince the media and the outdoors-oriented Minnesota citizenry that Lake Superior retained its pristine qualities despite the discoloration caused by agate-like tailings barely an inch thick on the lake floor. This was one of the first real-life situations that dramatically illustrated the economic tradeoff brought about by the resolution of an environmental dispute. Unless tailings could be inexpensively dumped in the lake, taconite was not economical. It was cheaper to import iron ore from Venezuela than to dispose of the tailings on land. When the federal court banned lake disposal, the taconite processing plant was closed leaving 3,000 employees without jobs in an area devoid of other economic opportunity.

For many years, Burson-Marsteller has had an outsized reputation for helping clients cope successfully with crisis situations. Many associate our crisis handling reputation to our work with Johnson & Johnson during the two Tylenol crises, the first in 1982 and the second in 1985. Certainly those highly visible engagements served to make Burson-Marsteller and crisis management near synonymous. But the fact is our first recognition for crisis management came a full decade earlier when we created for Owens-Corning Fiberglas (OC) a crisis simulation exercise known as "Bad Day at Black Rock." We got the assignment in 1972 after CEO Bill Boeschenstein tasked Jim Murphy, then OC's top public relations officer, with staging a community relations seminar for plant managers and their senior reports, a total audience of about sixty. Jim (now chief marketing officer at Accenture) called on B-M's Jim Dowling who, working closely with

Murphy, came up with an initiative called "Bad Day at Black Rock." CEO Boeschenstein's purpose in calling for a community relations meeting reflected his sensitivity to newly enacted legislation that mandated pollution abatement, non-discrimination in hiring and a host of other issues, including safety, that seriously impacted future business behavior.

Black Rock was a mythical community of 41,000 residents not unlike the small towns where actual Owens-Corning manufacturing facilities were located. Once predominantly rural, Black Rock had been so successful attracting industry that many of its citizens were moving to "exclusive planned communities" in a newly created suburban ring, complaining of "over-industrialization and bad zoning." Although the town "aristocracy" was still very much in charge, a new mayor had been elected on a reform platform and newly-formed special interest groups were becoming very vocal. Among them were recently organized chapters of the Sierra Club and NOW (National Organization for Women).

The problem-at-hand for purposes of the seminar was that Owens-Corning was about to undertake a significant facilities expansion at a time the company was perceived to have repeatedly acted in bad faith. While the expansion would add 200 new jobs, it required additional fuel oil storage tanks on a once historic site that was rezoned for industrial usage after OC purchased it. Also at issue was a variance to allow Owens-Corning to increase total on-site supplies of propane to levels exceeding building code limitations.

Owens-Corning managers were furnished a set of facts and formed teams to present their case to a town zoning board role-acted by Burson-Marsteller people. In a fast-developing scenario, a citizen lawsuit was filed charging Owens-Corning with withholding information on the true contents of the tanks. The local PTA protested the increased truck traffic as a hazard to young children, and talk of fiber glass health hazards began to circulate in the community. To complicate matters even more for OC, local radio stations were reporting that an atmospheric inversion kept smoke emissions and a noxious odor from dispersing. Other issues confronting OC managers included a sudden death at the plant, a meeting with Sierra Club representatives on environmental matters, a sex discrimination case brought by a female employee and a visit by a NOW delegation, at the time considered one of the most aggressive NGOs. These were issues addressed by the new legislation that affected Owens-Corning plant managers and support staff.

Response to the seminar was so positive that Boeschenstein ordered it repeated the next year. Manager attendees were uniformly in agreement that the format and content of the day-long program had increased their sensitivity to the new legislative and cultural environment. They also felt better equipped to analyze and deal with the issues in a rational manner. What might have been a dreary day-long presentation by a series of talking heads on such subjects as relating to community law enforcement authorities and how to support local public schools, instead had been turned into an exercise where an important segment of Owens-Corning's management structure had an opportunity to contribute and participate. Jim Murphy's intuition that "I wanted to do something different – something that would be memorable" paid off – "community relations" at the plant level had a new meaning at Owens-Corning.

For Burson-Marsteller, Black Rock had a near-magical effect on both the thirty-plus staffers who worked on the project and several hundred of their colleagues who later saw a condensed film version of the event. Black Rock was one of the first of many B-M-created "multi media" presentations utilizing from twenty-four to forty-eight carousel slide projectors and two to four motion picture projectors requiring a thousand or more 35-mm slides and extensive film footage. Black Rock won a PRSA Silver Anvil for Owens-Corning and Burson-Marsteller.

⸺ ◦≈≈◦ ⸺

Shortly after the "Bad Day at Black Rock" seminar, we were hired by Gulf Oil, then a major U.S. gasoline brand headquartered in Pittsburgh. CEO Bob Dorsey anticipated the kind of problems the petroleum industry would face with the growth of the environmental movement and the passage of new environmental and other social legislation. Dorsey wanted Gulf management – not only senior managers but also middle management wherever Gulf had installations – to be both forewarned and prepared.

My associates Buck Buchwald and Tom Mosser constructed a twelve-hour day-long session that evolved around a mythical town called Crisisport, a city of 650,000 people where Gulf was a major employer and the second largest taxpayer. In written materials provided to attendees (over the course of a year some 2,000 at multiple locations in the U.S., Latin America and Europe), Crisisport was described in meticulous detail: its governmental structure; political and social forces in the community; ethnic and religious composition; a description of Gulf facilities that included a refinery and petrochemical plant, a credit card processing center, operating oil wells nearby, a pipeline, marine terminal and other support structures.

About two hundred middle and senior managers attended each session after receiving a letter from CEO Dorsey transferring them for one day to a new Gulf facility at Crisisport. "During our day-long seminar you'll be asked to handle the full-range of public relations problems that a Gulf manager might be expected to encounter," his letter stated.

The program was in five parts.

The first was press relations and dealt with issues that might arise at any Gulf facility. Borrowing techniques used in the Owens-Corning Black Rock initiative, each attendee, a member of one of five working teams, received a mock newspaper front page whose lead article carried one of five headlines:

Gulf to Lay Off Number of Employees; Additional Reductions Forecast
Gulf Opposes Transportation Referendum
Proposed Offshore Well Will Fry Our Fish, Critics Say
Ex-Gulf Employee Spills the Oil Beans
O.C.A.W. Launches Plan to Unionize Gulf Operations Here

Their assignment was to develop a plan to react to these articles, not only a communications response but a policy determination affecting the issue reported on in the mock news article.

This was followed by dramatically staged role-played sketches in issues that were top of mind at that time: consumerism (reflecting consumer rights legislation recently passed by Congress); civil rights (newly-enacted legislation forbidding employment discrimination based on race, religion, gender, age and, later, marital status and sexual preference); pollution (Clean Air and Clean Water legislation had recently been enacted and the petroleum industry was perceived to be one the worst offenders). Teams were told they had "one week to prepare for a new pollution referendum" that would be discussed at a town council meeting. The challenge to team members was "what do you do?"

Another exercise in the scripted 140-page scenario was a catastrophic emergency that Gulf managers first learned about from this radio special bulletin while driving to work:

We interrupt this program to bring you a special bulletin from the WAWA newsroom:

An explosion at Gulf Oil's Crisisport refinery shook the city just moments ago and has left the giant Gulf complex in flames. Casualties are expected to be high with hundreds of workers on the grounds... Communities 30 miles from the site are reporting broken windows... There could be scores dead and many more injured.... There are hundreds of fuel storage tanks scattered across the Gulf complex and the fire is still raging out of control...

The final segment covered preparation for a TV interview which, before the advent of 24-hour business news channels, was still something of a novelty for business executives.

A letter from one participant, a mid-level manager in Gulf's Governmental Relations Department wrote what Crisisport meant to him:

Congratulations on Crisisport! It was the most well-prepared, well-documented, and best executed program I have ever attended...

...Crisisport made me more fully aware of the problems we in Gulf are facing today and gave me a lot of food for thought.

This program resulted in several adaptations for other oil companies including Amoco and Chevron and helped establish Burson-Marsteller's expertise in crisis preparedness and crisis management.

The Tylenol crisis is the one that Burson-Marsteller is most often associated with. Actually there were two Tylenol crises, the first in 1982 and the second in 1985. Whenever the subject arises – in media interviews and in Q&A sessions at schools of communications and other public relations groups – I quickly make the point that the real Tylenol hero was Jim Burke, Johnson & Johnson's CEO who took charge from Day One of both crises and stayed the course twenty-four hours a day – as did Larry Foster, J&J's highly capable and keenly astute public relations chief. Burson-Marsteller played a role, but as a member of a superb team that met daily around a large rectangular table in a conference room adjacent to Burke's office in New Brunswick, New Jersey.

The first crisis arose when seven people in a Chicago suburb died after taking Tylenol capsules. It was soon discovered that the capsules had come from Tylenol packages which had been removed from supermarket shelves and tampered with. Deadly cyanide was skillfully injected into individual capsules and the packages were returned to their original shelf space in pristine condition. Soon after the deaths were linked to Tylenol, news reports pointed to Tylenol's manufacturing plant in Pennsylvania as a possible source of the cyanide even though cyanide is not used in the manufacturing process. However, a small amount of the deadly chemical was present in a laboratory remote from the production line. This rumor was put to rest when J&J overrode a long-standing ban on cameras in their production facilities and allowed Dan Rather's CBS news crew to show how Tylenol is produced and packaged.

Although the name Johnson & Johnson does not appear on a Tylenol package, Burke quickly concluded the world would soon know that McNeill Laboratories, Tylenol's manufacturer, was a wholly-owned J&J subsidiary. He wisely concluded that the good name of Johnson & Johnson was at stake and immediately assumed the role of both crisis manager and corporate spokesman. We began working with Burke and Larry Foster after Ed Ney, then CEO of our parent company Young & Rubicam and Burke's close friend, suggested that Burson-Marsteller could help. Jim Dowling responded quickly. (I was in Paris at the time and returned several days later).

The key to the successful resolution of the issue was that CEO Jim Burke personally led the decision-making process. He grabbed the initiative by reaching out to the media, especially the evening TV network news programs that were then primary news sources for two-thirds of the American people. Burke projected a high degree of credibility and sensitivity on television, a major plus for Tylenol. Very probably, Burke's most effective attribute was his consistency in delivering the Tylenol message of responsibility to the customer and responsibility to the community, both heavily stressed in the Johnson & Johnson credo.

After it was established that a third-party had poisoned the capsules, J&J and Tylenol were regarded as victims of an evil act that threatened the safety of the nation's food and medicine supply – in fact, any product stacked unattended on supermarket shelves. Perhaps our boldest move was encouraging Burke to seek an interview with Mike Wallace on "60 Minutes." It was, I suspect, one of the rare instances when the CEO of a major corporation actively sought an appearance on "60 Minutes."

Even though the Food & Drug Administration never demanded a recall of Tylenol from all retail outlets, Burke decided to do so. It was an expensive decision – some estimates ran as high as $150 million – but it reassured customers of J&J's commitment to their well-being. For three months, Tylenol customers were forced to buy competing analgesics. When time came to reintroduce Tylenol in new tamper-resistant packaging, working closely with Larry Foster and J&J's internal public relations staff, we suggested that massive television, radio and local newspaper coverage was necessary to rekindle customer preference for Tylenol. Our reasoning was "most people learned about Tylenol's problems from hearing or reading the news and that's where they should get their information about the new repackaged Tylenol in a tamper-resistant carton." Our media experts believed that making Tylenol a local story in major markets would put the story on the front pages of local newspapers and make it the lead item on local TV news programs. What we believe to be the first nationwide satellite press conference accomplished this objective. At the time, this was a gee-whiz undertaking that rated a separate "sidebar" as a new way to hold a press conference and practically guaranteed coverage by local TV and newspaper reporters. Originating in New York, where national media turned out in droves, the press conference was beamed to thirty cities across the United States. As our media mavens predicted, the story led the evening TV news shows and made the front page, with photos, in most markets. The new-fangled technology that beamed a Waldorf-Astoria press conference to local downlinks was a major part of the story!

Unfortunately, there was a second act for Tylenol after three people died from swallowing poisoned Tylenol capsules purchased at a Bronxville, New York, supermarket. Again, Jim Burke took charge and used the Johnson & Johnson Credo as his guidebook. For the better part of two weeks, I was one of those around his conference room table. As with the first Tylenol crisis, Burke was a resolute leader – keen in his analysis, quick to make a decision – and invariably right. He occupies a special place in my pantheon of top CEOs I have worked with over the past half century.

After Tylenol, CEOs and public relations professionals alike linked Burson-Marsteller with crisis management. For a decade or more, our crisis business was fueled by telephone calls from executives in distress, as many as two or three in a single week. In dealing with most crises, our objective is usually to contain the crisis locally or regionally or, better still, to resolve the problem before it reaches the media. With more frequency than ever publicly acknowledged, heavily reported instances of commercial terrorism often inspire copycats. Shortly after the second Tylenol tampering in 1985, the CEO of a major canned goods marketer telephoned to set up an immediate meeting to discuss a blackmail threat. He told Jim Dowling and me that his company had received in the mail three cans of its principal product with a note saying the cans had been penetrated with cyanide. Company engineers were hard-pressed to locate the point of penetration, but on opening and testing one of the cans, they were able to verify the presence of the deadly poison. The author(s) of the note threatened to put cyanide-laced cans on store shelves in twenty markets unless the company followed instructions for delivering a large sum of money in small bills to a location yet to be designated. The company was in a crisis mode for a month when the perpetrators, very likely suspecting a trap, failed to pick up a large garbage bag stuffed with some currency and mostly waste paper at a designated remote mountain site. Although several Burson-Marsteller staffers stood watch around the clock until the issue was resolved, not a word appeared in the news. This was not a one-of-a-kind occurrence.

The day (December 3, 1984) *The New York Times* ran a front page story reporting on a devastating lethal explosion at a Union Carbide chemical facility in Bhopal, a hard-to-reach city in central India, we got a call from a senior Union Carbide executive at corporate headquarters in Danbury, Conn., asking for our help in disseminating information to the media and other affected audiences. Some 3,800 people died, 40 suffered permanent total disability and 2,680 permanent partial disability from the explosion and from inhaling noxious chemicals. A principal challenge for Union Carbide, which owned a 50.9 percent interest in the Indian business, was facilitating news coverage from the remote state of Madhya Pradesh before the widespread use of satellite communications. A team of B-M communicators flew immediately to Bhopal, John Birch, a Brit in B-M/New York, among them. John, as an officer in the British Army, had been stationed in India before joining B-M/London and subsequently heading B-M offices in Melbourne and Kuala Lumpur. He and other B-Mers remained in India for several weeks to gather information, feed it to corporate headquarters and cooperate with journalists who had traveled to Bhopal.

At the outset, media representatives were informed that Union Carbide was committed to disclosing what it knew about the explosion and the loss of life, and that a daily press briefing by a Union Carbide spokesperson would be held. A mechanism was set up for the Bhopal team to transmit information from the disaster site to a war room at Union Carbide corporate headquarters. For about a month journalists and TV crews from around the world attended Union Carbide's briefing at its Danbury complex. From the beginning, a single spokesperson was responsible for all communications with the media. Although this resulted in little sleep for the spokesperson, it assured the delivery of consistent messages to the media.

After consultation with Henry Kissinger, the former Secretary of State, and despite the hostile environment in India, we supported CEO Warren Anderson in his intention to demonstrate his personal concern and the concern of his company by visiting the site in India soon after the explosion. On his arrival in

Bhopal, Anderson was detained by state government authorities and kept, unharmed, under house arrest for several days. An upcoming state election was a likely factor in his arrest. But his visit gained him and Union Carbide considerable good will from media around the world. The fact that he was detained – a possibility that was considered but believed to be unlikely after an Indian government assurance of safe conduct – proved to be a plus from a public relations standpoint.

From time to time, Burson-Marsteller has been criticized for working for Union Carbide on the Bhopal disaster – seemingly (and illogically) linking us to the explosion and the huge loss of life. My response to this criticism has been that, by facilitating global press coverage, we assisted our client in performing a valuable public service and living up to its social responsibility.

Pan Am Airways reached out to Burson-Marsteller when its Flight 103 exploded over Lockerbie, a small village in Scotland, on the night of December 21, 1988, in history's first vicious terrorist aerial attack. Bound from Frankfurt via London to New York and Detroit, two hundred and fifty-nine passengers, including a number of Syracuse University students returning from year-end European holidays, lost their lives. An additional eleven Lockerbie residents were killed by falling debris. A team of B-M crisis and media professionals headed by Ray O'Rourke played a role in the massive communications task on both sides of the Atlantic. Recognizing the public perception that American commercial air lines – particularly Pan Am, the pioneer and largest trans-Atlantic carrier – were the likely targets of future terrorist attacks, our efforts centered on persuading travelers to and from overseas destinations that Pan Am, led by CEO Thomas Plaskett, was taking an aggressive proactive role in employing maximum security measures to protect passengers. But Lockerbie proved to be the beginning of the end for Pan Am – less than three years later, it was out of business, bankrupt.

Burson-Marsteller was a late arrival in the jumbo-sized legal battle between Goliath-like Texaco and David-like Pennzoil. They were engaged in a lawsuit that led to history's largest jury award, largest bankruptcy filing and largest cash settlement. We were hired in 1984 by Pennzoil CEO Hugh Liedtke who recognized that winning in the media could be as important as winning in the courtroom. The fact was that tiny Pennzoil's early judicial wins were being thrashed and discredited by giant Texaco's effective media relations campaign. Our mission was to level the public opinion playing field.

When the litigation ran its course and a federal district court jury awarded $10.5 billion to Pennzoil, the noted Harvard Law professor, Lawrence Tribe, attributed "substantial credit" for the victory to the favorable media treatment generated by Burson-Marsteller after joining the Pennzoil team. Our principal strategic contribution to the media coverage turnaround was persuading Pennzoil management to be aggressively proactive in communicating with the media and financial analysts. They had the better story all along; they simply weren't telling it.

Another major undertaking for Burson-Marsteller on the litigation front was helping Dow Corning defend itself in one of the largest class action suits ever undertaken. The suit was brought in 1992 on behalf of tens of thousands of women who had had breast implants over the past three decades. Our assignment embodied a classic example of coordinating a legal strategy with a public relations strategy. Unfortunately, Dow Corning managers and researchers in years past had generated numerous documents, many later taken out of context, that swayed the jury toward an adverse decision that was upheld on appeal. The $3 billion damage assessment led to the bankruptcy of Dow Corning (the company has since been reorganized and is once again a profitable business). Ironically, several reputable studies by leading medical organizations have shown that breast implants were not responsible for the immune system disorders claimed by the plaintiffs, and there is now a move afoot to regain FDA approval for the breast implant procedure.

Following the appeals court decision on breast implants, Burson-Marsteller was hired to work under the direction of a federal judge to notify claimants in more than seventy-five countries that they were entitled to a share of the proceeds from the suit. This was not our first such assignment. A few years earlier, we carried out a federal judge's order to notify claimants of their entitlement from a class action award to women who had used the Dalkon shield, a contraceptive device manufactured by the Robins Company. This, too, involved programs in many countries around the world. At the time, Burson-Marsteller was almost unique in possessing the global resources to implement a program of this kind. A third such assignment, in the mid-1990s, involved polyvinyl chloride (PCV) plumbing tubing.

Two (late 1960s/early 1970s) assignments I have remembered through the years: Texaco hired B-M/Brussels to plan and implement the May dedication/opening of a new petroleum refinery in Antwerp. This facility represented a huge financial commitment to the new European Common Market, and Texaco management expected major press coverage as well as attendance by some seven hundred European influentials, among them the King and Queen of Belgium. Many of the guests would be transported from Brussels to Antwerp and return on a chartered train. Our man-in-charge was Richard Newcomer, who had transferred to Brussels from B-M/Pittsburgh.

Newcomer was advised by his more experienced B-M/Brussels colleagues not to put too much reliance on the unpredictable Belgian weather. Accordingly, his plan included two enormous air-conditioned tents where guests would enjoy an elegant sit-down lunch. All went well until Texaco's CEO made a personal "final inspection" of the venue two days before the event. When he saw the pitched khaki-colored canvas tent tops in the foreground of his gleaming new refinery, he stared at his local pr director and our Dick Newcomer and bellowed "That won't do – those bare ugly tent tops." Whereupon Dick retorted, "But, sir, those tent tops are going to be covered with thousands and thousands of flowers, but I thought it would be too extravagant to order fresh flowers for your inspection visit – I can assure you they'll be there for the dedication ceremony."

When our client contact received a bill for our services and out-of-pocket expenses, he happily approved an unbudgeted $25,000 for thousands of fresh flowers that covered the ugly canvas tent tops.

The other (one in which I was personally involved) was once rather widely known among B-M and client insiders as the "itchy fanny" case history:

For some three decades before and after World War II, fiber glass was a popular drapery material. Fiber glass drapes came in a variety of colors and patterns, they hung well, they were durable and they were machine washable. Pre-WWII homemakers were schooled in their care – they knew they should never put fiber glass draperies in a washing machine with wearing apparel. For unknown reasons, this handy household hint did not find its way to their post-WWII counterparts.

This lack of knowledge manifest itself in what the media of the early 1970s characterized as "an epidemic of rashes" on female posteriors, at first a mystery illness but soon connected with fiber glass. Young homemakers were putting their fiber glass drapes and their undergarments in the same load of wash, and tiny, almost invisible, slivers of fiber glass attached themselves to the underwear, and from the underwear to the wearer's rear end. For a couple of months, the media had a lot of fun with the issue, especially the cartoonists, i.e. "what mother failed to tell her daughter." Both local and national columnists couldn't resist writing (and offering advice) about what one commentator described as a "medical phenomenon." Even a few newspapers carried editorials, one on the wisdom passed (or not passed) from one generation to another.

The solution seemed easy — simply put a warning label on the draperies instructing homemakers to wash them separately from wearing apparel. But that presented a problem: our client Owens-Corning did not make the draperies. In fact they were two steps removed. They made the glass fibers that were woven by a manufacturer who supplied the fabric from which the draperies were made by still another manufacturer. Ultimately, however, warning labels began appearing on fiber glass drapes, but they were somewhat of an afterthought. "Itchy fannies" by then were so much in the news that just about every homemaker could tell you that fiber glass drapes and underwear should never be in the same load of wash.

Chapter 11

❦

The Olympic Games: A Quarter-Century Relationship

The Burson-Marsteller relationship with the Olympic movement dates back a quarter of a century. It started with the Los Angeles Summer Olympic Games in 1984 and continues to the present. Central to the relationship has been a two-decade association with the United States Olympic Committee. In addition, we have worked with a score of Olympic corporate sponsors – for some, like Coca-Cola and McDonald's, repeatedly at summer and winter venues. On a personal level, I count my involvement with the USOC, much of it pro bono, among the most satisfying of my roles as a public relations professional. Mike Moran, John Krimsky, Harvey Schiller, Bill Hybl and the late Robert Helmick have been both good clients and good friends.

————— ❧ —————

We entered the world of the Olympics almost by accident. For the better part of a decade starting in the 1970s, I had courted AT&T – both PR vice president Paul Lund and his successor, Ed Block, after Paul's untimely death from lung cancer in 1975. I yearned to have that great name on our client list. Opportunity knocked when I got a telephone call from Andy Cooper, a long-time B-Mer then responsible for our consumer group in New York. I was at a Friday off-site senior management meeting when Andy related that Carol Schumacher, one of our most effective client service managers, had, by chance, learned from one our competitors that AT&T was going to sponsor the Olympic Torch Relay and was in the process of selecting a public relations firm to work with them. Andy was aware that I knew Ed Block. I telephoned Ed and asked him for the opportunity to present our credentials. Ed told me that several agencies had already presented, but he would see what could be done to accommodate us. He called back within the hour and told me we could present, but that all the agencies on their list already having done so, we would have to present the following Monday. With B-M's entire senior management elsewhere, Andy took command, put together a team, brainstormed over the weekend, put together the presentation and met with the AT&T selection committee on Monday. Before the end of the week, AT&T informed us we would be their public relations partner in implementing the AT&T Olympic Torch Relay.

Thus began perhaps the largest, certainly most logistically complex, project ever undertaken by Burson-Marsteller. More than one hundred and sixty B-Mers helped implement the cross-country run from United Nations Plaza in New York City across the length and breadth of the continental U.S. to Memorial Stadium in Los Angeles. The event required twelve thousand runners who carried the Olympic Torch eight thousand miles through thirty states. The original flame, according to custom, was ignited on Mount Olympus in Greece. It was flown to Kennedy Airport in New York and trucked to United Nations Plaza where the AT&T Torch Relay officially began on May 8. It then took a circuitous route across the vast expanse of our country. The flame from one torch lighting the next, kilometer-after-kilometer, until it finally reached the huge natural gas-fueled cauldron atop the Olympic stadium. One destination along the route was the south lawn of The White House and President Reagan personally welcomed the torch entourage. Literally scores of events involving governors and mayors marked other stops, each meticulously planned in advance. One of the most painstaking aspects of the project was organizing media events scheduled to the exact minute in scores of cities, towns and villages over a two-month time frame. At the opening ceremonies for the XXIst Olympiad, the torch was carried into the stadium by a granddaughter of the legendary Olympic Gold Medal track star, Jesse Owens. Until entering the stadium, the torch bearer's identity was a well-kept secret.

Thousands of hours went into planning the Olympic Torch Relay, with Tom Mosser, Nick Kilsby, Al Schreiber, Steve Aiello and, of course, Andy Cooper playing prominent roles on the B-M team. Each day's progress was carefully mapped to maximize attendance and media coverage. The support team during the actual run consisted of a caravan of some twenty vehicles that transported medical, food preparation, security, media and government relations, communications and other staff to assure uninterrupted progress of the torch. A B-M advance team preceded the torch by 24 to 48 hours to make certain all arrangements for media coverage were in order. Scheduled to-the-minute, there was seldom any deviation and the torch reached the Olympic opening ceremonies within sixty seconds of the scheduled time.

A major obstacle that had to be overcome was recruiting torch bearers in unpopulated areas, mainly west of the Mississippi River. Most runners were people who "bought a kilometer" for $1,000 with the funds going to Boys and Girls Clubs and YMCAs and YWCAs in the donor's area. In sparsely peopled areas, AT&T's retiree organization, The Telephone Pioneers of America, recruited volunteers and transported them to points along the relay route where one runner would pass the flaming torch to another. They included all manner of people, young and old, men and women, boys and girls, people of diverse ethnic backgrounds, all representative of the communities along the relay path. During each of the nine weeks of the Torch Relay, at least one national network evening news program reported on its progress and *USA Today* published a daily map tracking its route.

AT&T was one of more than a half-dozen major Olympic sponsors Burson-Marsteller represented during the 1984 Olympics, others including M&M/Mars, Coca-Cola, Westinghouse and Flying Tigers. For Mars the games were the centerpiece of a global recognition program for employees (in the Mars culture, they are called "associates"). For two years Mars associates competed for points toward an all-expense trip to the Olympics. We handled all the logistics including housing, food and transportation to the numerous venues in and around Los Angeles. For the four days they were at the Games, three groups of four hundred Mars associates lived in fraternity and sorority houses on the University of Southern California campus within walking distance of many of the events. One of our people, knowing that these houses were vacant during the summer months, came up with the idea to rent them for client use during the Olympics. Mark Bain, who now heads corporate communications for Alticor (formerly Amway) was transferred from B-M/NY to B-M/Los Angeles to direct on-site Olympic activities for B-M clients.

The relationships we developed during the Los Angeles games set the stage and heightened our desire and resolve to continue our association with the Olympic community. In particular, I was determined that Burson-Marsteller have a role in the 1988 Summer Games in Seoul, Korea. Having had minimal contact with Korea even though we had operated in Asia more than a decade, I engaged my friend, Philip Habib, recently retired from the Foreign Service after achieving the rank of undersecretary for political affairs at the State Department, to facilitate my visit to Seoul in November 1984. Habib was the U.S. ambassador to Korea in the 1970s and one of the Americans most admired by Koreans. He arranged a meeting for me with the Seoul Olympic Organizing Committee, many of whom were his long-time friends. The head of the committee (SLOOC) was the former Korean army commander, General Roh Tae-woo, who later became Korea's first elected president. We learned we had won the business in early 1985 (Hill & Knowlton was our principal competition). Our assignment was to assure the world that Korea had the resources and determination to stage the 1988 Summer Games in a manner consistent with previous Olympiads in a secure environment and the world's most advanced sports facilities. In short, Burson-Marsteller was to be Korea's voice to the world. In fact, Korea was on its way to becoming a world class nation. Already it was among the top dozen trading nations.

One of my best decisions was choosing Bill Rylance to be our on-site liaison with SLOOC's Secretary-General, Park Seh-jik, who had succeeded Roh Tae-woo. Bill was twenty-eight years old when he arrived in Seoul, his first visit to the Orient. He had been with Burson-Marsteller three years, starting in London and then moving to Bahrain. Bob Leaf had brought him to my attention. Bill soon recruited Bryan Matthews, an Asian-based correspondent for London's Daily Mail, and the two of them spent the next three years implementing a broad-ranging program for the 1988 Seoul Games that included specific agendas in the United States, Japan, the United Kingdom, Germany, France and Spain – all countries important to Korea. Bill and Bryan served as a "mini-secretariat" for the head of SLOOC, participating in many international policy matters and conferences, writing speeches and responding to international inquiries. Among the more interesting initiatives was developing and implementing a strategy to assure Soviet Union participation in the Seoul Games. At the time, Korea and the U.S.S.R. did not have formal diplomatic relations and the Soviet Union had boycotted the Los Angeles Games. Working with Tass correspondents based in

Tokyo, Burson-Marsteller facilitated the initial exchange of messages between the two countries. U.S.S.R. participation in the Seoul Games is credited with the speedy establishment of diplomatic relations between the two countries, somewhat similar to the Korean relationship with the People Republic of China. To facilitate media coverage during the games, we imported some twenty B-Mers from a dozen countries to help manage the Olympic Press Center and serve as interpreters for overseas journalists.

Bill Rylance and Bryan Matthews left Burson-Marsteller after the completion of our contract with SLOOC at the end of 1988 and established Merit Public Relations in Seoul. B-M acquired Merit at the turn of the century and Bill Rylance subsequently moved to Hong Kong as CEO of Burson-Marsteller Asia/Pacific operations. Bryan Matthews remained in Seoul as B-M's senior representative in North Asia.

Another group of B-Mers half-a-world away were engaged in another major Olympic-related activity. B-M/Oslo was recruited in 1983 to help Lillehammer, a small Norwegian ski resort, develop a strategy and program to win the venue competition for the Winter Olympic Games in 1992. A team headed by Per Heggenes and including Kai Henricksen and Trond Andresen worked almost five years preparing submissions to the International Olympic Committee and persuading IOC members and other Olympic influentials that an unknown village in Norway, some seventy miles north of Oslo, was the ideal site. According to Per Heggenes, "The aim of the communications program at the early stages was in three parts: to make the candidacy known, to make it credible, and finally, and very important, to establish good relations with those we later defined as the real decision-makers and those who identify with them."

The B-M team took a leading role preparing the Lillehammer presentation to the IOC in Calgary in 1985. The first of three elements was a multimedia presentation titled "In this we believe." It highlighted Lillehammer's natural qualifications for being the venue as well as how completely Norway – its people, its lifestyle, its culture – reflected the Olympic ideal. The second element was labeled "The Challenge." It described the resources Lillehammer could bring to bear to so huge an undertaking. Interestingly, parallels were drawn to how the Norwegian government and private sector overcame the challenges brought about by the successful Norwegian offshore oil drilling initiative.

Finally, a document titled "The Facts" was a three-volume, five hundred page detailed account of all the information a member of the IOC required to be fully conversant with Lillehammer's bid. Despite this enormous effort that included personal contact with IOC members as well as the individual sports federations and national governing bodies, Lillehammer failed to get a majority of the votes. Albertville, France, was selected as venue for the 1992 Winter Games.

The Lillehammer Organizing Committee decided immediately to continue its quest for the venue in 1994 (several years earlier, the IOC voted to abandon the practice of holding the Summer Games and the Winter Games during the same year every four years; instead the Winter Games are now held midway between the Summer Games). Having once experienced the competitive process, Lillehammer entered the competition with a greater degree of confidence. It sharpened its messages to IOC members and other targeted members of the Olympic community. There were five in all:

- Lillehammer was the only venue where all sports events, excepting alpine, could take place within walking distance of hotels and other lodging.
- All the required facilities were already finished or under construction, irrespective of the IOC decision.
- Lillehammer offers ideal and predictable climate conditions for winter sports.
- Norway's tradition of and commitment to winter sports (No. 2 to the Soviet Union in winter Olympic medals, 1.7 million of its 4 million inhabitants are members of the Norwegian Confederation of Sports).
- The establishment of a permanent Scandinavian winter sports center if Lillehammer was the Winter Olympic venue.

Coincidentally for me and my B-M associates, the IOC meeting to vote on the 1994 venue took place during the Seoul Summer Games in September 1988. Persevering to the very end of the process, the Lillehammer organizing committee enlisted the Prime Minister of Norway to demonstrate her nation's commitment to the Olympic spirit with a personal appeal to the members of the IOC immediately before the vote was taken. This strategy worked – Lillehammer was an easy winner. I learned about it soon after the vote while having lunch with John Krimsky, the USOC's deputy executive director and chief fundraiser, at the Seoul Intercontinental Hotel, a stone's throw from the magnificent Korean Olympic complex. Kai Hendriksen thought (correctly!) that I would like to know the good news.

Olympic sponsorships came of age at the 1984 Los Angeles Summer Games when Peter Ueberroth recruited corporate sponsors in some two dozen categories at $4 million each for exclusive rights to use the Olympic rings. Barely two decades later, the cost of a global category exclusive sponsorship (a TOP sponsor) has risen to up to $40 million – with some twenty-plus takers for the 2000 Sydney Summer Games.

My observation through the years is that most sponsors – Coca-Cola, McDonald's, Visa and Kodak are exceptions – fail to take full advantage of their sponsorships. They pay big bucks to the IOC for the sponsorship, let two years idle by and then decide they lack funding for a promotion/publicity budget that would cost them a couple million dollars.

During most of the time he was the non-paid volunteer president of the U.S. Olympic Committee, I was a close confidant and adviser to Robert Helmick. Bob was a successful Des Moines lawyer whose special expertise was in tax-free bonds issued by states, municipalities and other government entities. His rapid rise in the Olympic movement started when he became chairman of U.S. Water Polo in 1969 and a member of the board and executive committee of the Los Angeles Organizing Committee in 1979. A dedicated and passionate believer in the Olympic movement, he was elected a USOC vice president in 1981. Four years later he was elected USOC president which, for him, became a near full-time occupation. The same year he was elected to the IOC and four years later he was appointed to the IOC executive committee.

I met Bob at a USOC reception at the 1984 Summer Games in Los Angeles and took an immediate liking to him. His commitment to the Olympic movement was infectious and following his election as USOC president I offered him my support. He asked me to be a member of the USOC marketing and public relations advisory committee, headed by Olympic fencer Edgar House. Bob was a frequent visitor to New York and my advisory role evolved from our lunches together and his many visits to my office. My unwritten briefly spoken agreement with him was that I personally would serve him in an advisory capacity without compensation. I told Bob I preferred a personal pro bono arrangement because I wanted to feel absolutely unimpeded in telling him exactly how I felt on any given issue. I believed working as an unpaid free agent would facilitate that objective and best serve Olympic interests.

In late August 1991 Mike Moran, the USOC's highly regarded public relations chief, telephoned to give me a "heads up" on a story being pursued by *USA TODAY*, one of the few American newspapers that regularly reports on the Olympics. The gist of the story was that Bob Helmick was alleged to have a conflict of interest in that while serving as USOC president, he was representing clients seeking to influence the USOC. I had an appointment with Bob the next day and asked him if the story were true. He admitted representing several clients, but fiercely maintained he had done nothing that compromised his role as USOC president. After relating to me his conversation with the *USA TODAY* reporter, he sought my advice on what could be done to soften or neutralize the story that was likely to result from his interview. Based on my conversation with Mike Moran, it seemed clear to me that *USA TODAY* had the story and no good purpose would be served by talking further to their reporter. Before telling that to Bob, however, I asked him the direct question "do you have any other clients, beyond those known to *USA TODAY*, whose business interests are Olympic-related?" I volunteered that, if so, it would be better for him if everything came out in one story. I said the worst-case scenario for him would be for further conflicts to be discovered one-by-one and result in a series of adverse articles that would then be picked up by other media. Bob assured me that "no other shoes would be dropping" – or words to that effect.

The *USA TODAY* report, published September 6 – a full-page in the Sports section under the banner "Inside the USOC: A Look at Its President"– cited four situations where Helmick was perceived to have a conflict. (Helmick admitted to having the relationships.) The clients were Turner Broadcasting, sponsor of the Goodwill Games, which Helmick as USOC president at first strongly opposed but later supported; Saatchi & Saatchi, the advertising agency on retainer to USOC to sell sponsorships; the Director of Marketing for the U.S. Golf Federation which had applied to USOC to become golf's national governing body; and an organization hired by Brunswick Corporation to help bowling become an Olympic sport. The article appeared on a Friday, the day before a scheduled meeting of the USOC Executive Committee.

Although Bob Helmick publicly pleaded that he had not used his office to further the interests of his clients (which, beyond providing access to decision-makers, I have always believed to be true), he faced near-universal condemnation – from reporters who regularly covered the Olympics and from throughout the Olympic community. Largely, the argument was that perception equated to reality and on that score, he had harmed the USOC.

The day the story broke in *USA TODAY*, Bob and I met to assess the damage. He was resolute in wanting to retain his position as president and had prepared a list of arguments supporting his actions, among them that "the rules of the USOC clearly permit me to undertake legal engagements related to sport" and "I have been providing legal and counseling services similar to these since 1977." Out of our discussion came the idea that he would inform the USOC Executive Committee that he would not seek re-election after the Barcelona Olympics about ten months hence. While I regarded it as a desperation measure not likely to satisfy his critics, I did not discourage him. The executive committee's response was the appointment of a special counsel (Arnold I. Burns, former U.S. deputy attorney general) who was tasked to assure the executive committee that Helmick had made full disclosure of his representations which could be perceived to be in conflict with his responsibilities as USOC president.

During the next week, *USA TODAY* revealed that Helmick had additional relationships with clients seeking to influence USOC or IOC. He had misled the USOC Executive Committee, he had misled me and he had misled the media. If Bob had any chance of serving his term through the Barcelona games before the new revelations came to light (I believe that was a possibility if he had admitted everything from the outset), it seemed to me now that he had only two options: either to resign or to be forced out of office.

Helmick was alone in defending himself. We spoke by telephone several times a day as the media, fueled by adverse comments from within the Olympic family, continued to thrash him and the USOC. Some columnists called for his resignation. This was a heart-wrenching painful experience for him and I suffered alongside him throughout the ordeal. During his next visit to New York on September 18, I told him that I had concluded he would best serve the Olympic movement by resigning. By then, he was so beaten down by the media pile-on that he accepted my recommendation without protest. In fact, I recall him asking only "do I have to resign from the IOC also?" While I believed that was inevitable, I suggested he take it one step at a time and await IOC developments, pending its meeting the first week in December. As he sat facing me in my office, I showed him the handwritten five-paragraph resignation statement I had scribbled in red pencil hours before our meeting. His eyes misted as he read it and he accepted it without change. I would be less than candid if I failed to admit that I dropped a tear or two while escorting him to the elevator.

Prior to the IOC meeting in Lausanne, Bob spoke with me several times about strategies which might allow him to remain on the IOC board. Foremost in his mind was whether he should arrive a day or so early for a private meeting with Antonio Samaranch, the powerful IOC secretary-general. I favored such a meeting because I felt that the IOC would follow Samaranch's will. Bob asked if it made sense for me to accompany him to Switzerland and I told him I thought that could be counter-productive and did not offer to go with him. Rather, I assured him I would stand by for his telephone calls if he wanted to talk or seek advice. Helmick's presence at the IOC meeting was greeted with a hailstorm of adverse articles in newspapers in Britain and on the Continent, all citing the conflict issue and many equating it to a breakdown in integrity that affected the Olympics worldwide. He got no support from his fellow IOC members.

He called me from Lausanne the evening after the opening session as I was leaving the office about six o'clock New York time – midnight his time. He asked for my counsel. I told him I thought he should resign gracefully – otherwise, he risked expulsion by the IOC which, I thought, would have been far more damaging to him – and, collaterally, to the USOC. He asked me to write a resignation statement. I didn't tell him, but I had already done so. I told him it would be FAX'd to his hotel within the next quarter hour. I waited ten minutes before sending it. Sadly, that was the last time Bob Helmick and I spoke.

With the passage of time – and Bob's death in early 2003 – there has been speculation on whether it was really necessary for Bob to resign since the USOC investigation reported in late November 1991 – a good two months after the media storm started – that he had not abused his office. I counseled him to resign because of the rapid erosion of confidence in the USOC at a critical moment in the Olympic time cycle – less than a year from the start of the Barcelona Summer games. My reasoning was that the media showed no signs of letting up and a continuing barrage of adverse news coverage would seriously undermine USOC programs like training and sponsor relationships. I continue to believe I did what was best for the USOC and for the Olympic movement worldwide – in suggesting both his resignation from the USOC and the IOC – even though I continue to think kindly of him. While I feel certain he spoke with others about whether he should resign – and that his direction may have already been decided on the two occasions when I provided him with a written resignation statement – it is worth noting that he sought no additional advice after talking with me. In both instances, he made public his resignation in a matter of hours after he had the written statements in hand. Throughout this tragic episode, I purposely avoided contact with any other USOC or IOC officers or directors.

For the record, the USOC investigation report concluded:

"We have found no evidence that Mr. Helmick influenced, or attempted to influence, any USOC officers, directors or staff members in connection with their consideration or approval of contracts or transactions involving Mr. Helmick's private clients."

To summarize from the view point of a public relations professional: this is a classic example that demonstrates the role that perception plays in influencing attitudes and behavior.

Chapter 12

$\approx$

Summing Up: My Thirty-five Years as CEO

Most likely, I may not have made it as CEO of the Burson-Marsteller of the 21st Century. For all the thirty-five years (1953-1988) I was Chief Executive Officer, I lived with the naïve notion that doing good work for clients in a happy work environment would deliver the wherewithal to reward and retain our people, grow the business and provide an acceptable profit to our employee-shareowners. While that simple formula worked for me, I know, that alone would not work today.

The public relations consulting business has changed since I was CEO – starting about the time Jim Dowling succeeded me in 1989. The business environment is harsher, more competitive – one which most likely would not nurture a repetition of the Burson-Marsteller story. The fact is, I have often thought how lucky I was from a timing standpoint – setting up a public relations firm after World War II. The years that followed were glory years for the business, for Burson-Marsteller and for me.

As I wrote in an earlier chapter, I believe Burson-Marsteller's single most defining moment was launching an office in Europe in 1961 with the intent of eventually establishing a global presence. At the time, Hill & Knowlton was the only

U.S. agency with overseas capability. An Australian firm, Eric White & Associates, acquired by H&K in the early 1970s, had an Asian network and an office in London, but was unknown in the U.S. For three decades, Hill & Knowlton and Burson-Marsteller had minimal big league competition outside the U.S. (the U.K., Canada and Australia were exceptions). It was a time when American companies were becoming aware of the need for public relations to establish themselves in new markets where they were often totally unknown. As we had hoped when deciding to go to Europe, numerous overseas clients later engaged us in the U.S. Moreover, despite the startup costs launching new offices, our overseas operations were profitable and growing rapidly.

That economic nirvana (for us and H&K) began to change in the late 1980s as large advertising agencies began to acquire public relations firms. The first was in 1978 when Foote Cone & Belding bought Carl Byoir Associates, the third largest firm, behind H&K and B-M. It should be noted that this transaction represented the second round of interest in public relations by the large advertising agencies. Shortly after World War II, Foote Cone went into public relations in a big way (for that time), followed by McCann-Erickson with its Infoplan international public relations subsidiary; and Benton and Bowles with General Public Relations. In the early 1960s, these advertising agencies abandoned their public relations units because they were unable to operate them profitably and, on several occasions, unsatisfactory public relations performance put major advertising accounts at risk.

I think I am on solid ground in observing that Burson-Marsteller played a major role in renewing the ad agencies' interest in public relations. Our relationship with Marsteller Advertising demonstrated that an advertising agency (at its peak, Marsteller was the eighteenth largest) and a public relations firm could productively coexist. And, second, that a public relations business could be sizeable as well as profitable (in 1979 our fee income was $28 million and our margins were in the high teens even after contributing to a profit-sharing retirement trust). In the 1960s and 1970s I regularly attended the annual meetings of the American Association of Advertising Agencies with Bill Marsteller. The heads of all the large agencies were there, and year-after-year one or more took Bill and me aside to talk merger, their main objective being to establish a strong foothold in public relations. Of the ten largest agencies of that era, nine wanted to acquire us.

In 1979, the year that Bill had repeatedly said he would retire, I thought the time was right for the combined Marsteller Advertising/Burson-Marsteller to join up with one of the major agencies. In this, I was encouraged by two of our independent board members, Joe Wilkerson, a Young & Rubicam retiree, and Bill McNeill, our long-time legal counsel. There were three reasons. First, I thought a big agency could hasten the transformation of Marsteller Advertising into a consumer agency, a goal that eluded us for more than a decade despite effective work for major clients (including two commercials that are in the Museum of Television and Radio all-time top fifty). Second, I was concerned our existing business would not generate enough cash to finance Burson-Marsteller's rapid expansion. And third, as our public relations business overtook the advertising agency in income and profits, tensions among senior officers of both businesses began to develop – that was a problem I did not want to deal with after Bill's retirement.

Shortly after the start of the new year, I told Bill I thought the business would be best served by being acquired by one of our suitors. I wanted the transaction to be completed before he retired. He said he thought it would be the wrong way to go. He asked me to think about it for sixty days and we would talk again. Meanwhile, he spoke with Joe Wilkerson and Bill O'Neill. They knew our business and our people and Bill regarded them highly. In early March I told Bill I had not changed my mind. While he still had reservations, he said he would support my proposal to team up with a suitable partner. My choice of that partner had been made long before I raised the issue with him. At that time I was much closer to the advertising business than in recent years and knew the senior officers of almost all the big agencies. In my book, Y&R was at the top of the heap. Moreover, Y&R's CEO Ed Ney had aggressively pursued us for almost ten years.

Bill wisely noted we would lose negotiating leverage if Y&R knew we were talking only with them. He suggested we identify another potential purchaser and negotiate with the two simultaneously. We chose the second agency by each writing a name on a sheet of paper, a practice we had followed in resolving a number of issues. We both wrote "Ogilvy & Mather," in large part because we admired Jock Elliott, O&M's CEO, and knew the next two ranking officers. For the next ten weeks or so, we met many times with Ed Ney and his cohorts and with Jock Elliott and his team. Both were intensely interested in acquiring us. Our goal was to get the best deal for our shareholders (though I continued to prefer Y&R as a future partner). We were seeking cash and stock (cash for retiring shareholders and other employee/owners who wanted cash and shares for those who wanted a tax-free exchange). Ogilvy, already a listed company on the New York Stock Exchange, had recently acquired a "hot" mid-sized agency, Scali Sloves McCabe, and was cash short and their stock offer didn't meet our expectations. In July, we and Y&R jointly announced our merger effective October 1, 1979. Bill retired December 31 and was succeeded by Dick Christian, his long-time number two in our advertising business. From that point onward, Marsteller Advertising and Burson-Marsteller began to emerge as two distinct entities. Burson-Marsteller revenues for 1979, the last year we were independent, were $28.3 million; in 1983, the year we became the world's largest public relations firm, our revenues were $63.8 million.

The news that Young & Rubicam acquired Burson-Marsteller energized other big agencies to follow suit. In May 1980, J. Walter Thompson. which had long offered product publicity services, notably in New York and London, acquired Hill & Knowlton. Ogilvy, which had committed to public relations by acquiring a boutique public utility specialist firm prior to our talks, began to build a broader public relations presence. Barely a decade later, nine of the top ten public relations firms were owned by advertising agencies or large communications groups. Of the major public relations firms, only Edelman and Ruder·Finn have remained privately owned.

One fallout of the takeovers by big ad agencies was that these once U.S.-centered public relations firms began to expand overseas – seemingly wherever B-M and H&K had dots on the map. Bankrolled by their new owners, they embarked on buying binges to establish themselves in Europe, Asia, Australia and Latin America (what Australia needed least was more public relations firms!). At the same time, an entrepreneurial Brit named Peter Gummer began assembling a global public relations giant named Shandwick, later acquired by Interpublic, the last of the communications giants to embrace public relations. The effect of this expansion was quickly intensified competition for new business, with reduced fees often the deciding factor. Also, competition for qualified staff grew as these newcomers sought to upgrade service to satisfy multinational clients. It was only natural for them to turn to Burson-Marsteller and Hill & Knowlton for safe hires. The result has been profit erosion in most overseas markets. A good example is Singapore, one of our most consistently high-margin offices when a single international firm was our main competitor. With a half dozen major firms now chasing business in a relatively static market, profits are not nearly as robust.

———— ❦ ————

During my final year as CEO, we brought together members of Burson-Marsteller's senior management team, about seventy-five men (mostly) and women representing our operations on five continents. About three-fourths were at Burson-Marsteller for more than fifteen years. Few of them had been with B-M less than five years. Today, the same kind of meeting, whether ours or a meeting of a principal competitor, would be peopled with managers with considerably less tenure. The fact is, young people entering the professional services workforce no longer commit themselves to lifetime employment with a single firm. People like Elias Buchwald with fifty years, Bob Leaf and Al Smith with forty years, Claude Marshall and Chris Fisher with thirty-five years, Jim Dowling and John La Sage with thirty years, Martin Langford with thirty years at four offices, Peter Walford with twenty-five years at four offices — that kind of commitment to one company is increasingly a relic of the past. A staff comprising so many talented individuals, working together decade after decade, was a critical component of Burson-Marsteller's success. We knew one another's strengths; we knew one another's weaknesses. We became better together than we were one-by-one.

The nature of the relationship between a client and its public relations firm has changed (the same applies equally to law firms). While I was CEO the client-agency relationship, especially among *FORTUNE* 500-size companies, was based mainly on trust and the close personal association of the client's chief executive officer and most senior public relations officer with the agency's top people. Admittedly, the larger public relations firms were then much smaller than their counterparts today and so were typical client companies. Once selected as "agency of record," a public relations firm could expect to provide all services the client required under the rubric of public relations. As corporations decentralized and established multiple well-defined profit centers, that model changed. Increasingly, profit center managers chose public relations firms of their choice. Indeed, at some major consumer product and pharmaceutical companies, individual brand managers select public relations firms. It is not unusual for a large multinational firm to employ a dozen or more public relations firms around the world – or even in the United States alone. In our early days it would have been "bad form" for a retainer client to seek proposals from other public relations firms for specific projects. In fact, there was a time if a client had asked us to compete with a competitor for a project, we may have resigned the business.

Still another change involves what I call "the work flow." In days past, we and our clients jointly prepared an annual public relations program – strategies and initiatives that supported CEO business objectives – short-term and long-term.

We addressed the client's weaknesses with initiatives aimed to gain more favorable public understanding and reinforce client strengths. We were fully informed of major new product introductions, changes in marketing strategy, potential acquisitions and divestitures, changes in management structure or personnel and other matters likely to impact public reputation and perception. Plans responding to all such issues were incorporated in the annual program we usually started preparing in October for review and acceptance before the end of the calendar year. An annual budget covering service fees and out-of-pocket expenses was an important element of the planning process and enabled us to know with a fairly high degree of certitude our income for the next year. The approved budget was usually the minimum revenue we could expect from a client. Unplanned events called for monies in addition to budget. During business downturns, however, we could expect budget reductions although business-to-business clients often reduced their much larger advertising expenditures and increased public relations.

Nowadays, a significant fraction of the revenue of most large public relations firms comes from ad hoc projects for which they are hired to implement as the year unfolds. It is, therefore, more difficult to forecast annual income. Most of the larger firms derive most of their income from hourly charges for specified units of work. The result is that the larger firms especially expend more effort and money chasing new business. This not only diverts staff from servicing clients, but also eats into profits. At the start of the calendar year, a firm like Burson-Marsteller will usually have commitments for about two-thirds of its budgeted revenue at the start of their fiscal year. The remainder, which would represent the total income of a top ten agency, must be sold as the year progresses.

⸙

A pressure I never encountered as CEO was managing a significant business unit of a company whose shares were publicly traded. I view myself as having been blessed for being a member of a management that could set and live with its own financial expectations. Today's model for the large public relations firms and their parent communication groups calls for producing financial results that accord with stock market expectations. The punishment for failing to reach goals can be severe.

This does not mean that we were financially undisciplined during the twenty-six years we and Marsteller Advertising did business in tandem or the eighteen "pre-going-public" years we were a member of the Young & Rubicam family. As part of Marsteller, we had a rather simplistic financial objective we called "the rule of fifteen." It was Bill Marsteller's idea and it sounded good to me when I first learned about it. Moreover, it worked! Our objective was to grow fifteen percent a year and earn an after-tax profit that returned fifteen percent on equity after paying fifteen percent of covered salaries into a profit-sharing retirement fund. We measured our results on a five-year rolling average and were never below target.

The years have reaffirmed to me how valuable people are to a service business like public relations. From the beginning, I hoped that people we hired would make Burson-Marsteller their lifetime career destination and many did just that. But if I had the luxury of reliving my business life, I would pay even more attention to recruiting, training and development, motivating and rewarding our people – even though I suspect we did about as good a job at it as anyone in our line of business.

During our first fifteen years when we served mainly business-to-business clients, our "ideal hire" was a graduate engineer with journalism experience, invariably a white male. We mined the good trade magazines – published by McGraw-Hill, Chilton, Penton and Cahners – and a few business-to-business corporations like General Electric and Union Carbide, which had strong internal public relations departments and good training programs. Frequently, one hire would lead to numerous others like when Bill Noonan joined us from Union Carbide in the early1960s and was soon followed by Sam McCracken, Claude Marshall and Don Jeka, all of whom stayed with us more than twenty years. Our first female hire for a professional position, Lynn Waplington, was in 1968. Lynn majored in chemistry and worked for one of the large chemical companies. We had won the Enjay Chemical account (Exxon's chemical subsidiary) and needed account people with chemical experience. Hiring a woman staffer was not only a rarity at Burson-Marsteller but for all public relations firms and corporate departments other than those engaged in food, fashion, cosmetics or houseware publicity. Our original intent was to utilize Lynn's talents for "inside" tasks like writing, editing, programming and, perhaps, placing articles in the trade press. The press of work for Enjay, however, soon had Lynn not only calling on the client but also visiting client customers seeking case history material for articles in chemical magazines. Lynn was a productive member of the Burson-Marsteller staff for twenty years and left to head public relations for the Christian Science Church in Boston.

Having Burson-Marsteller on a resume is arguably the best credential a candidate for a public relations position can hope for. We laid the groundwork for that reputation early on. For fifteen years, Buck Buchwald and I shared responsibility for hiring new people. We both interviewed just about every professional staffer. As in other aspects of the business, I was the "good cop" and Buck was the "bad cop." But we were usually single-minded on staff performance: our people were either making it or not; there was seldom any middle ground. Later we often joked about what we thought was our surefire way of predicting whether a new hire would "make it." We stood unseen close to the open office door of the newly employed person and listened to the cadence of the typewriter keys. When we heard a steady clackety-clack, we knew we had a winner. When the cadence was belabored, one stroke at a time, we had reason for concern. After a few months, recently-hired employees were told whether or not they were succeeding. Those not working to our standard were advised to seek other employment. It didn't take long for the buzz to get around that Burson-Marsteller "blew a fast whistle." That, I believe, accounted in great measure for our popularity with search firms as a fertile recruiting source. It has become almost axiomatic, even to the present day, that a person who has worked three or four years at Burson-Marsteller must be good; otherwise, they would not have lasted that long.

Until the end of the decade of the 1980s, many, if not most, of our people were recruited from the media. Nowadays, few, other than those from television news, have had media experience. Two reasons account for the change. Public relations firms no longer offer journalists enough of a salary differential. When people of my generation left a newspaper or magazine for a public relations job, either agency or corporate, they could expect an income boost of thirty percent or more (my salary doubled when I moved from a newspaper job to public relations – $25 to $50 a week!). Newspapers, magazines and press associations now pay as well or better than public relations firms at lower and mid-staff levels. A second reason is today's journalists seem to believe working for the media carries with it a purity that's compromised in public relations. Accordingly, few working journalists now actively seek public relations jobs. But because working with media to place and develop stories is so central to public relations, this presents a problem for our business. It accounts to some considerable extent for the complaint often voiced by reporters and editors of a lack of understanding of the news media and the news process by public relations people. Since these complaints have escalated in recent years, it is reasonable to assume that one cause is the declining number of former journalists now engaged in public relations.

As conditions in the marketplace and employee attitudes have changed, I have marveled at how intensely former employees remain committed to Burson-Marsteller even after having departed many years earlier. It's difficult to point to any one factor that accounts for this continued loyalty. Primary among them, however, is that almost from the beginning, and certainly starting in the 1960s, Burson-Marsteller has been an exciting place to work. Not only did we grow rapidly, we had an early start accumulating a blue chip client list of pace-setting companies committed to public relations. For decades, hardly a day passes in any part of the world that a Burson-Marsteller client is not in the news. For those B-Mers who demonstrated they could take on more responsibility, promotions came fast and so did increased salaries and bonuses. In reality, when a public relations firm, in fact any service business, grows at double digit rates, high profitability is almost inevitable. It's simply not possible to hire staff fast enough to service the incoming flow of new business. What happens is that existing staff is forced to work, nights, weekends and holidays – and the irony is, they invariably love it. The excitement of being part of a successful enterprise seems to compensate for intrusions in time that would be devoted to personal or family matters. Admittedly, we made mistakes promoting some people to jobs which they were not capable of handling. When that happened, we usually created another job for the person who didn't make it, a practice that caught up with us when forced to reduce overhead by the industry-wide recession in the early 1990s. Many of those "other" jobs were largely "make work" positions we could afford during our growth surge. We considered the cost minimal when measured against the cultural environment we sought to foster.

<hr />

My view on new business has always been rather simplistic. Nothing attracts new business faster than being able to offer a client superior talent. Existing clients are the first to respond. It never fails that they broaden the relationship with new projects. Subsequently, non-clients learn of the good work either by word-of-mouth (which is epidemic throughout the public relations community) and by observation (they see it in print or on the electronic media). Through the years I have observed that the really effective "hires" are soon discovered – first by their co-workers and later by clients. Regardless of their position in the organizational hierarchy, they soon become fully billable. In truth, sad to say, those possessing "star" quality are limited in any organization, profit or not-for-profit, client or agency, service business or otherwise. But I have always felt that we at Burson-Marsteller had more than our share of them as compared to our competitors.

Burson-Marsteller had a consistent low key new business program when I was CEO, our first ten years or so excepted. During that first decade when we were almost literally starting our business from ground zero, we systematically talked with most Marsteller Advertising clients. Other than Rockwell or Clark, clients before Burson-Marsteller became a formal entity, about a dozen signed on with us, generally at our minimum fee of $1,000/month with the proviso that time costs in excess of that amount would be billed to the client. More often than not with Marsteller's mid-sized advertising clients, hiring a public relations firm was a new experience. Our presentations explained the role of public relations in the marketing mix as well as our special credentials. Probably because of our links to an advertising agency, B-M presentations were usually more sprightly than those of competitors. For example, we were early users of Carousel projectors and had a case history library of 35-mm slides. Early on we set a minimum annual growth goal of fifteen percent with half derived from increased client budgets and the remainder from new clients. For the three decades-plus, we exceeded our objective. At internal management and training meetings, expanding existing client budgets was always a priority agenda subject and client budget growth was recognized and applauded.

Among our most productive new business people were hands-on middle managers leading accounts day-to-day. They carried the title, client service manager, and were one of three or four others with the same title who reported to a group manager (a title somewhat equivalent with today's office practice leader). Our New York office, always our largest, had eight to twelve groups of thirty to sixty people in the 1970s and 1980s, while Chicago, then our second largest office, had four to six groups. Client service managers were evaluated on their ability to "sell" clients new projects or new services producing increased revenue. Some of them – Larry Snoddon (Merrill Lynch), Tom Mosser (Burger King), Jim Dowling and Bill Noonan (Owens-Corning) – made their reputations doing this. Clients like Merrill Lynch and Owens-Corning started at the hundred thousand dollar level and grew into multi-million dollar accounts (for many years, Merrill Lynch and Owens-Corning alternated as our largest single client with budgets in the $3 to $4 million range).

General managers were responsible for "growing" their offices – which translated into bringing in new business and growing budgets of existing clients. They were assisted by an informal cadre of specialists that included the likes of Buck

Buchwald and Tony Hughes when having an engineer or a financial specialist on the new business team was needed to prove to a potential client that we knew his business. For years, hardly a month passed without my participation in a new business presentation assuring the prospect that his/her business was important to Burson-Marsteller. John La Sage, long-time B-M general manager in Chicago who devoted a large part of his time to new business, was especially adept at utilizing our widespread resources cultivating and winning new business. His example was emulated in other offices in the United States and in Europe and in Asia. But the reality is that in the two decades starting with the 1970s, more new business came to us because of our reputation than from our prospecting.

The public relations "grapevine" was well-wired long before the advent of the Internet and e-mail. Reputations of individuals as well as firms – good, bad and mediocre – are quickly established and communicated throughout the relatively small but compact public relations community. We worked hard at establishing an identity with audiences we wanted to reach – corporations and the media. For the better part of twenty years our half-column ad appeared in the weekly newsletter of New York's Overseas Press Club, an active gathering point for reporters and editors and some public relations leaders in New York. Each ad featured a Burson-Marsteller client with a brief description of the client's business and a tag line that Burson-Marsteller provided public relations services to that organization as well as other leading corporations and business entities.

But our principal promotional vehicle was a distinctively-designed four page quarterly letter titled "The Burson-Marsteller Report" that made its debut in 1965. Our purpose in publishing it was to inform the business community that Burson-Marsteller was more than a business-to-business industrial publicity firm. Although I cannot remember ever hearing the term back then, we were beginning the process of repositioning ourselves. The content consisted of one lengthy article on a topical issue and a half dozen shorter items of significance to CEOs and public relations executives. Early representative titles of lead articles were: "The Student Rebellion - Who Speaks for Business on the Campus?"; "Problems in Prosperity - How to Protect the Consumer Without Punishing the Producer"; "Pollution in Paradise - The Time Has Come for Industry to Make its Position Clear"; "Big Government vs. Big Business - How to Keep the Powers in Balance"; "Keeping Company Secrets - Questions for Management."

The Burson-Marsteller Report appeared for almost twenty years and developed readership in the public relations community that elicited up to twenty letters after each issue. Four thousand copies were sent to CEOs and public relations executives, mainly the *FORTUNE* 500 list, as well as editors, government officials and other influentials. The publication's popularity was largely a factor of its superb writing by Richard L. Bode, a B-M account executive who later authored several novels. The content came from input from Buck Buchwald, Dick Bode and me. Each of us was on the lookout for our next lead topic, and we met a couple of times before each issue for up to four hours fleshing out the lead article. Shorter items were usually inspired by an article one of us had seen in another publication. I believe our reputation for being "strategic" was strongly reinforced by the "The Burson-Marsteller Report." We discontinued the publication after Dick Bode left to join the *Reader's Digest* as a staff writer. Four issues appeared following his departure, each by a different writer. None in my view were up to Bode's standard and I thought it better to stop publishing.

This is my final chapter on Burson-Marsteller as it was during the thirty-five years I headed the organization. It coincides with the completion of our 50th Anniversary Year. If you have been a careful reader, you may have observed that my ruminations have included little about the company since 1988 other than the new offices we opened. I have purposely avoided commenting on or second-guessing my successors as CEO.

Essentially, my objective has been to make this a personal memoir in which the pronoun "I" has, for me, been used rather profusely, for which you have my apology. However, I am quick to repeat that I fully acknowledge that the Burson-Marsteller I described reflects the efforts, intelligence and commitment of literally hundreds and hundreds of men and women in some thirty-five countries on five continents. For many of them, Burson-Marsteller was central to their professional lives and I will be eternally grateful to them for their commitment. Having my name "in front of the hyphen" has brought me both pride and satisfaction. Based on the response over the past year, mainly in the form of e-mails after each of the separate installments of what became this book, it is gratifying indeed to know that so many of you share that pride and satisfaction. That is the richest of all rewards.

A Closing Footnote

The publication of this book coincides with my eighty-third birthday. That I continue to "go the office" every day seems to me only natural. It's the only life I know or want.

Working alongside Chris Komisarjevsky the past five-plus years has been a special treat. He is a solid public relations professional, a good executive and a thoroughly decent human being. Every day, he makes me feel welcome and wanted and I am most grateful.

— Harold Burson
February 2004